PROTESTATION RETURNS

1641-1642

and other contemporary listings:

Collection in Aid of Distressed Protestants in Ireland;
Subsidies; Poll Tax; Assessment or Grant;
Vow and Covenant; Solemn League and Covenant

Compiled by

Jeremy Gibson and Alan Dell

With a Foreword by

David J. Johnson
Clerk of the Records, House of Lords

Federation of Family History Societies Publications Ltd.

Published 1995 by
Federation of Family History Societies Publications Ltd.
c/o Benson Room, Birmingham & Midland Institute, Margaret Street,
Birmingham B3 3BS, U.K.

Copyright © Federation of Family History Societies Publications Ltd. on behalf of the compilers,
Jeremy Gibson and Alan Dell, 1995.

ISBN 1 86006 006 4

929.3 G18

Cover illustration: Detail from 'La manière et ordre de la Scéance de la maison basse ou des communes qui consiste en chevaliers gentils hommes et bourgeois' ['The manner and order of the session of the Lower House...'], c.1623, Sutherland Collection, Department of Western Art, Ashmolean Museum, Oxford (neg. Cl 318), reproduced by permission. This appears to be the only contemporary picture of the pre-Civil War House of Commons in session.

Computer typesetting, layout and cartography by Jeremy Gibson.
Printed by Parchment (Oxford) Limited.

Acknowledgments

Our first thanks must go to David Johnson, Clerk of the Records, House of Lords, for his Foreword, and for the courteous and friendly assistance provided by his staff, whilst examining the Protestation Returns. To this is added his last minute contribution of previously unsuspected Poll Tax certificates for Lincolnshire and Staffordshire.

At the Public Record Office hundreds if not thousands of rolls in E 179 were examined; we are most grateful to the staff who had to produce these, as well as to Susan Lumas who facilitated their production and Dr David Crook for his advice and support. Cliff Webb researched the records of the Collection in Aid of Distressed Protestants in Ireland, in E 179 and SP 28; he has generously allowed us to use the information in the list he prepared.

Although most of the records are in national repositories, local archivists were circulated and as usual replied helpfully to our enquiries. It is to be hoped that this Guide will encourage acquisition of microform or photocopies so that records can be studied locally and wear and tear on the documents (as well as researchers) can be reduced to a minimum.

This Guide has been in preparation for several years, during which time we have been helped by a number of individuals who have our thanks: Stella Colwell, for advice on the taxes of the period and provision of the schedule of county quotas forming Appendix Two (page 15); Duncan Harrington, for Kent parishes with covenants; Cecil Humphery-Smith, who loaned his transcript of the early published list of protestation returns; Beryl Hurley, for help with Wiltshire hundreds and placenames; 'the other' David Johnson (stalwart of the F.F.H.S.), for lending us his copy of Nottinghamshire Protestation Returns; Professor Margaret Spufford, for reading the Introduction and making helpful suggestions; and Dr T.L. Stoate, who together with the late Bill Webster, did much to make the protestation returns more easily available; also, finally, our printers, Parchment (Oxford) Ltd., for the light table, and Stuart Cope, of Johnsons of Witney, for his patience and expertise with the map reductions.

                                                                    J.S.W.G. and A.D.

Federation of Family History Societies Publications Ltd. is a wholly owned subsidiary of
the Federation of Family History Societies, Registered Charity No. 1038721.

CONTENTS

FOREWORD

Amongst the records of Parliament there is always the possibility that the name of an individual may appear - as a petitioner or witness, or as subject of a bill, appeal, question or committee enquiry - but there are scarcely any of those lists of names - of taxpayers, householders or parishioners - which are the stock-in-trade of genealogists. Administrative returns are the business of government, including local government, not of Parliament. Almost the only such sources in the House of Lords Record Office are the Protestation Returns (and a few Poll Tax Certificates).

That so many Protestation Returns should have been made - they survive for almost one third of the parishes in England - is surprising since the wording was always controversial. Though the Protestation was aimed specifically at the perceived popish threat, some Anglicans feared (rightly) that their own liturgy and church government were under attack. Indeed, in January 1641/2, sheets of the Protestation were being used as banners by Parliament's more rowdy supporters. Furthermore, the taking of the Protestation was authorised by no more than a resolution of the House of Commons (on 30th July and 2nd August 1641) and by the Speaker's letter (of 20th January 1641/2); in July 1641 the House of Lords had rejected a bill which would have legally imposed the Protestation on the whole country.

The uniqueness of the Protestation Returns makes them difficult to compare with other 'censuses'. Nevertheless, by studying them together with the other, virtually contemporary, listings described in this Guide, it should be possible to draw valid conclusions about people and places in the 1640s, a demographically obscure period before the Hearth Tax Returns of 1662 and subsequent years.

The only finding aid hitherto available has been the list compiled by the Royal Commission on Historical Manuscripts in 1876. This has proved very reliable and will still be necessary to locate particular returns. The present Guide, with its corrections and annotations and with the addition of lists of 'Collection', taxation and other records, will open up these fascinating documents to a wider audience. I marvel that so much information can be conveyed in so compact a form and look forward to welcolming many more students of our seventeenth-century ancestors.*

David J. Johnson,
Clerk of the Records,
House of Lords.

---

* The House of Lords Record Office is open to the public, by prior appointment, from 9 a.m. to 5 p.m., Monday to Friday (Bank Holidays excepted).
Intending searchers should write to the Clerk of the Records, Record Office, House of Lords, London SW1A 0PW. Tel.: 0171-219 3074 (telephone), 2570 (fax).
The Protestation Returns are available on microfilm, forming part of the House of Lords records marketed as *Politics and Statecraft in Early Modern England*, Pt. 2, from Primary Source Media, 50 Milford Road, Reading RG1 8LJ (tel. 01734 583247).

INTRODUCTION

Nearly all the records listed in this Guide relate to 1641 and 1642, generated in the tense months preceding and during the start of the Civil War.

The *Protestation*, a form of oath of loyalty, ostensibly to the King, but in fact to Parliament, was initiated in the House of Commons in May 1641, when Members themselves took it. Nine months later its scope was vastly widened, when instructions went out that it should be taken by every adult (male); very occasionally women were also recorded. Closely associated with the Protestation was the *Collection in Aid of Distressed Protestants in Ireland*. The oath was taken and the collection made, often simultaneously, in February 1641/2 and March.

Parliament-approved taxation records recommence, after Charles I's eleven years of personal rule, with Tudor-type *Subsidies*, to be collected during 1641. In July 1641 a *Poll Tax* was voted, but few records of this survive. Thirdly, an *Assessment* or *Grant* was agreed, to be collected in May and November 1642. This Assessment had a much lower tax threshold and consequently many more taxpayers are named.

Whilst these three groups, *Protestation*, *Collection* and *Taxation* records, provide the most important sources (in the Guide), which have been researched in some detail, the far fewer records of the previous decade and the following years of Civil War and Commonwealth have been included when they have come to our notice, in particular the occasional published lists.

Historical background

In 1628 the third Parliament of Charles I passed the Petition of Right, whose first article declared that loans and taxes without the consent of Parliament were illegal. The Petition received reluctant royal consent, though the King subsequently violated all its articles. In the second session (1629), the House of Commons, with the Speaker held down in his chair and the doors locked, passed Sir John Eliot's 'Three Resolutions', which declared that whoever proposed innovations in religion, and whoever proposed or paid taxes without the consent of Parliament, was an enemy to the kingdom and a betrayer of liberties. These resolutions - combining the grievances which the House of Commons felt in religion and politics - were the last that the third Parliament was to pass, for it was at once dissolved. The next eleven years saw no Parliament - the longest interval England has known in her history since Parliament began - known as the years of Charles I's personal rule (or 'The Eleven Years' Tyranny').

This historical background is essential for an understanding of this Guide. For researchers, no Parliament effectively means no detailed records of taxation. Paradoxically, these eleven years produced what is one of the most notorious attempts at taxation, 'Ship Money', levied, without Parliamentary authority, from the mid-1630's on. Unfortunately, for researchers, its tax threshold was high, and its records meagre.

It was not until 1640 that the two disastrous Scottish Wars forced the King to raise money by taxation and thus summon Parliament again. It was the second of these, the famous 'Long Parliament', which was to legislate for the taxes and initiate the oaths and collections details of whose records, mostly over the two years from February 1640/1 to December 1642, comprise this Guide. These were crucial months when King and Parliament irrevocably parted company. To researchers whose main interest is in the names and status of those appearing in the records, or the sums they paid, quite when the taxes they were paying, the oaths they were subscribing to, became solely Parliamentary rather than 'King and Parliament', is of little relevance, but it is important to recognise the background, not least in the intention of many of these records to discover (and tax heavily) those who were recusants.

Rightly the best known of these are the *Protestation Returns* of February 1641/2 and March. Where they survive they provide the nearest there is (for the next two hundred years) to a widespread census of adult males. Much less well-known is the *Collection in Aid of Distressed Protestants in Ireland*. This voluntary collection was being made at the same time as people were taking the Protestation oath. Where lists of both survive they provide valuable corroboration or comparison. Where one is missing, the other goes a long way to providing a replacement.

It is significant that once Parliament was fully in control of the taxation system the tax threshold became much lower. The *Subsidies*, with their medieval origins and, despite Tudor efforts, subsequent ossification, taxed only the better-off. The *Assessments*, from 1642 on, initiated by a Parliament free of royal control and keen to raise as much money as possible, have a much lower tax threshold. This is good news for researchers, as the extant tax Assessments of 1642 can list up to seven times as many taxpayers as the Subsidies a year earlier.

The Protestation Returns

These returns owe their existence to the unrest which prevailed in Parliament during the passage of the Bill for Attainder of the Earl of Strafford in 1641. Most published transcripts include accounts of the events which led to the drafting of the Protestation and its taking by Members of the House of Commons and by peers, in May 1641. Although the intention was that all Englishmen should take the Protestation, this happened immediately only in a few parishes (see City of London). Instructions implementing this only became effective with a letter from the Speaker of the House of Commons to sheriffs the following January (1641/2) [for the Protestation and this letter see Appendix One, pp. 13-14]. Organised by hundred or (in the north-east) wapentake, ministers, churchwardens, constables and overseers of the poor were to take the Protestation before justices of the peace at a local market town. Lists of these officials not infrequently are extant, and their existence is shown. The officials then supervised the taking of the Protestation by their parishioners. Comparison of their names in the two lists is a salutary reminder of the diversity of spelling.

The returns were sent in to Westminster during March. One of the principal objects of the Protestation, defending the Protestant Religion against all Popery, was to discover the number of Roman Catholics in the country. On 16th April a House of Commons committee was appointed to consider what action might be taken against recusants, but the outbreak of the Civil War negated any further proceedings.

The original returns that were sent in are now in the House of Lords Record Office. By a fortunate quirk of fate, although they must have been sent in to the House of Commons, they ended up amongst the House of Lords records in the Jewel Tower, and so escaped the fire of 1834 which destroyed the Commons' archives. Their survival, geographically, varies greatly, as below (published complete returns in *italics*, partial publication asterisked):

Counties with near complete coverage: *Cornwall,* Cumberland, *Devon, Dorset, Durham, Huntingdonshire,* Middlesex* (excl. London), *Nottinghamshire.*

Counties with partial (but substantial) coverage: Berkshire*, Kent, Lancashire*, Lincolnshire, Oxfordshire, Somerset, Sussex, Westmorland.

Counties with slight coverage or isolated returns: Buckinghamshire, Cambridgeshire, Cheshire, Essex, Hampshire, Hertfordshire, *Northumberland,* Shropshire, Staffordshire, *Surrey,* Warwickshire, *Wiltshire,* Worcestershire, Yorkshire: North Riding, West Riding*; *Wales:* Denbighshire.

Counties with no returns: Bedfordshire, Bristol, Derbyshire, Gloucestershire, Herefordshire, Leicestershire, London, Norfolk, Northamptonshire, Rutland, Suffolk, Yorkshire: East Riding; *Wales* (incl. Monmouthshire) except for Denbighshire.

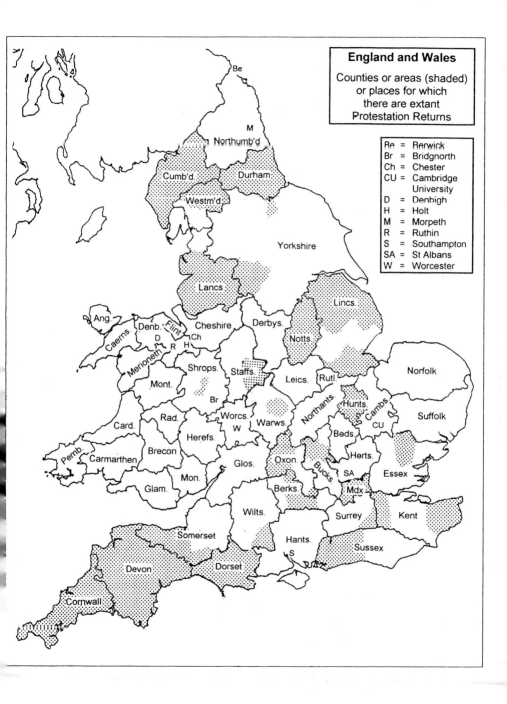

England and Wales

Counties or areas (shaded)
or places for which
there are extant
Protestation Returns

Be	=	Berwick
Br	=	Bridgnorth
Ch	=	Chester
CU	=	Cambridge University
D	=	Denbigh
H	=	Holt
M	=	Morpeth
R	=	Ruthin
S	=	Southampton
SA	=	St Albans
W	=	Worcester

Despite the very partial extant coverage at the House of Lords R.O., the Protestation appears to have been taken countrywide, in England at least, as occasional parish registers record lists of those participating, when returns do not survive (see also under the Collection, page 10). They sometimes predate the proclamation of January 1641/2 (see page 6). These local holdings are included in this Guide whenever reported, but there are probably more such stray survivals, details of which will be welcomed.

The importance of the returns was realised well over a century ago, and the places covered were meticulously listed in 1876 in the *Fifth report of the Royal Commission on Historical Manuscripts*, Part One. Report and appendix (C.1432), H.M.S.O., pages 120-134. Amazingly, there has been no reprint let alone a revised version of this list since, though the *Guide to the Records of Parliament*, by Maurice Bond (1971), pp. 154-55, lists, by county, extant hundreds and boroughs. Subsequently L.W. Lawson-Edwards produced a helpful checklist of printed and other sources, published in the *Genealogists' Magazine*, vol. 19 (1977), pp. 84-85, and as an offprint.

Most textbooks and other sources suggest these returns are of signatures, and many imply they include all over the age of eighteen. This may have been the intention, but is very seldom the case. The original returns at the House of Lords R.O. have all been examined for the purpose of this Guide. Most returns are on separate leaves of paper, or folded folios, for individual places. In southern counties, these will normally be parishes, though chapelries or hamlets may be recorded separately. In the north, where parishes may be vast and comprise a number of townships, these may have one return divided into sections, or have separate returns for different places. Returns of this nature have mostly been guarded and bound into volumes, arranged by county and hundred, though many of those for Lancashire, on very long parchment membranes, have been preserved differently. Some returns for a group of parishes have been transcribed together, for instance the Salisbury Division of Wiltshire, the City of Worcester, and in the West Riding of Yorkshire.

The vast majority of such returns are in one hand, that of the parson or parish clerk, though there will normally be signatures of the parson and (often marks) of churchwardens, constables and overseers. Returns with signatures and the marks of those unable to sign are indicated in this Guide by a dagger (†). In rural parishes it is unusual for more than two or three to be able to sign their names, though there are huge variations from place to place. A very detailed survey of those rare returns which have signatures and marks has been made by David Cressy, in *Literacy and the Social Order* (1980), pp. 65-68. This includes a table showing the number of such returns per county, and percentages of those signing or making their mark. Unfortunately, apart from Cornwall, such returns are usually few in number, so the conclusions drawn cannot be conclusive. If the rare survivals are typical then the percentages will be valid, but statisticians would probably dismiss these as being based on far too slight a coverage. In particular, the towns, where literacy is sure to be higher, are often missing from the returns entirely, and when they are extant, are almost always in a single hand. It is also important to emphasise that such returns only indicate the ability to sign one's name in an educated manner. Those making marks were unable to write, but that doesn't mean they couldn't read. Unlike the present day, reading was taught quite separately from, and long before, writing. By the age this was considered, seven and upwards, the children of the poor were often scaring birds.

The inclusion of women is even rarer. Again these have been indicated, usually by §. Sometimes women are in a separate list, sometimes intermingled with the men, sometimes in family groups, and sometimes mentioned but not named ('and his wife', 'et uxor'). Occupations are very occasionally given, particularly in Lancashire. Addingham in Cumberland, uniquely, provides ages.

The spread of returns showing signatures and marks, or a significant number of signatures, compared with the number of places extant, and women, is tabulated:

English counties, showing total parishes/places, number of Protestation Returns extant, those with signatures and marks, those mentioning women, and number of Collections in Aid of Distressed Protestants in Ireland.

County	Pars.	Prot	S&M	W	Coll.	County	Pars.	Prot.	S&M	W	Coll.
Beds.	127	(1)	-	-	55	N'hants.	292	(6)	-	-	5
Berks.	162	101	15	1	49	N'humbd.	80	2	0	0	0
Bucks.	206	57	4	8	132	Notts.	223	271	50	2	0
Cambs.	171	Univ.	0	0	1	Oxon.	234	100	0	0	0
Cheshire	130	8	1	0	2	Rutland	50	0	-	-	22
Cornwall	204	167	124	2	1	Salop.	229	12	0	0	49
Cumbd.	144	106	1	19	0	Som.	486	164	4	7	8
Devon	468	412	27	0	0	Staffs.	183	58	4	0	5
Dorset	260	239	11	0	88	Suffolk	482	(2)	-	-	0
Durham	94	80	0	0	0	Surrey	146	24	19	0	58
Essex	405	43	1	3	0	Sussex	305	158	27	0	168
Glos.	347	0	-	-	9	Warw.	208	19	0	0	1
Hants.	307	5	0	0	11	Westmd.	73	31	7	0	0
Herefs.	184	0	-	-	0	Wilts.	318	90	0	0	217
Herts.	132	5	1	0	85	Worcs.	209	9	0	0	2
Hunts.	132	85	27	0	10	York	30	(3)	-	-	17
Kent	400	91	2	0	160	Yorks ER	220	0	-	-	0
Lancs.	-	285	0	31	0	Yorks NR	231	11	1	3	0
Leics.	256	(4)	-	-	66	Yorks WR	261	130	0	0	0
Lincs.	627	374	50	5	38	**Wales:**					
London	102	0	-	-	71	Denbighs.	-	3	0	0	0
Middx.	67	60	3	1	37	Pembs.	140	0	-	-	3
Norfolk	691	(1)	-	-	245						

The figures for total parishes in the county and number of places with Protestation Returns or Collections are perforce approximate. Parishes may include chapelries, or they may be counted separately. In Lancashire parishes often comprise many townships. Individual returns are often to places rather than complete parishes, so, as in Notts., these can exceed the number of parishes in the county. Protestation Returns are at the House of Lords R.O. unless shown in brackets, which are isolated examples from parish registers.

Cressy has made a similar examination of the returns, and in an appendix lists places which met his strict criteria for providing evidence of literacy. They do not coincide exactly with those indicated here, as I have included all that appear to show signatures and marks.

The Collection in Aid of Distressed Protestants in Ireland

In the autumn of 1641 rebellion had broken out in Ireland. Thousands of Protestant 'planters' were massacred, thousands more fled to the fortified garrison towns or to England. There was an urgent need to provide emergency relief to the refugees, and to pay for a punitive force to suppress the rebellion. The traditional system of taxation, the Subsidy, was slow to collect and always produced far less cash than anticipated (see bolow). Parliament and King, in a rare moment of unity against what they saw as a common enemy, passed (on 31st January 1641/2) an emergency act to receive loans and free gifts for these purposes - though the military aspect was not emphasised as the charitable was. This Act (16 Charles I c. 30), 'for a speedie Contribucon and loan towards the releife of His Majesty's distressed Subjects of the Kingdome of Ireland' (the word 'Protestants' appears in the preamble), was designed to raise £400,000 but in the event only just over one-tenth of this figure was obtained.

The Act's importance to researchers is that the churchwardens, overseers and, ultimately, sheriffs, charged with collecting the gifts were also charged with submitting the names and contributions of the donors. The Act even instructed that these returns were to be printed and published, though, hardly surprisingly in view of the immediately succeeding national strife, this was never done.

Many of the returns do survive, however, in the Public Record Office, split between classes E 179 and SP 28 (mainly pieces 191-195). These have been examined in detail by Cliff Webb, who published an article outlining the number of parishes (or places) surviving for each English county (in comparison with the Protestation Returns) in the *Genealogists' Magazine* (vol. 21, no. 9, March 1985). He also prepared a list, by county, of the actual places for which there were returns. This information is, with his permission, incorporated in this Guide, though rearranged within each county by hundred. The rearrangement shows that often, as with the Protestation, it is returns for specific hundreds which survive, others being totally missing; but also, there are scattered places which reached the national records when their neighbours are missing.

The first to be published were in *Buckinghamshire Contributions for Ireland 1642...*, ed. John Wilson, Buckinghamshire Record Society 21 (1983), whose introduction remains the most substantial discussion of this record. The Act itself is printed as an appendix. Sadly the opportunity was missed of printing in parallel the Protestation Returns which are extant for Buckingham and Cottesloe Hundreds. What this important pioneering edition brings out is the very close association of Protestation and Collection. In ten places, in two separate hundreds, the preamble states that those listed 'have taken the Protestation and have contributed to the distressed Protestants...', the returns clearly having a dual purpose. Interestingly, returns for these two hundreds are not extant at the House of Lords R.O.

In contrast, the *East Sussex contributors to the relief of Irish Protestants 1642*, comp. M.J. Burchall (Sussex Genealogical Centre, Occasional Paper No. 10, 1984), mainly taken in April 1642, appear to have no such link with the Protestation. The only other Collection to have been published to date is that for Surrey.

Thus some Buckinghamshire Protestation Returns have ended up in the P.R.O. as part of the Collection records, but Collections for two places in Lincolnshire, Greatford and Wilsthorpe, listed on the same pieces of paper as the Protestation, are at the House of Lords R.O. Whilst no other Protestation Returns include Collections, it may well be that other records of Collections include, as in Buckinghamshire, Protestations as well.

As stated, the records of the Collection are mostly in E 179 or SP 28/191-195. They include (SP 28/195) a bundle of returns from unidentified parishes, some of which have been identified by Cliff Webb. However it is not unlikely that other stray returns are to be discovered in other SP 28 pieces (Stratford upon Avon has been found in SP 28/136).

The lists of contributors to the Collection, where they duplicate extant Protestation Returns, provide interesting though not uniform comparisons. In Buckinghamshire the Protestation might record from fifty to a hundred per cent more taking the Protestation, with evidence suggesting the Collection was restricted to ratepaying householders. Even so the latter contains contains some six times the number of entries as contemporary Lay Subsidies. In the Surrey Collections, one or two parishes seem to list all adult males, whether they gave or not, whilst others include gifts from women and even children. Two Surrey lists actually contain more names than the Protestations for those parishes. Others have only one-third the number of names in the Collections as in the Protestations. The Surrey evidence over the fourteen parishes with coverage duplicated in both records is that the Protestations contain 967 names and the Collections 630, which is comparable with the Buckinghamshire average. However, many names appear in the Collections which do not in the Protestations and *vice versa*, but, at least in Surrey, there is a high variation. In most some sixty per cent in the Collections are duplicated in the Protestation, two parishes rising as high as ninety per cent. It is to be hoped that more of the Collections will be transcribed and published, where possible with comparison with Protestation Returns.

The Covenants and Petitions to Parliament

In 1643 there were two further opportunities for loyalty to be shown to Parliament and the protestant church. The first was the *Vow and Covenant* introduced in the Commons on 6th June 1643, with instructions given on 27th June for organising the Vow in the localities. A further declaration, the *Solemn League and Covenant*, was agreed on 14th September 1643, which was being taken in London soon afterwards. By 30th January 1643/4 there was agreement that it would be 'tendered to all men within the several parishes above the age of eighteen, as well lodgers and inhabitants', and they were all to 'subscribe their names in the book or roll with their neighbours'.

Unfortunately there was no national collection of such subscriptions, which in any case were probably only taken in strongly parliamentarian areas. They are occasionally found in parish records, and are included here when they have come to notice, though no special search has been made.

In these years there were also numerous petitions to Parliament. One, from Somerset (1641), has been transcribed (page 64). The Remonstrance from Cheshire (1641), in the British Library, apparently royalist in sympathy, is another (page 23). However, no attempt has been made to research and catalogue these.

Taxation records

As mentioned earlier, the King's need of money to pay for the Scottish wars forced him to abandon his lengthy period of personal rule and summon Parliament: first, in April 1640, the Short Parliament, which lasted only three weeks; and, after the disastrous Second Bishops' War, in November 1640, what became known as the Long Parliament.

Thus in 1641 and 1642 three methods of direct taxation were adopted: a Tudor type subsidy, a poll tax and a fixed assessment or grant of a type which was later to become common during the Commonwealth period and in the reign of Charles II. The records engendered by these are in the Public Record Office in class E 179.

Subsidy. This was passed in December 1640, and approved by the King in February 1640/1: an Act for the relief of His Majesty's army and the northern parts of the Kingdom (16 Charles I c.2), granting four entire subsidies in two separate payments, the first by 27th February 1640/1 and the second by 15th April 1641. This was immediately followed by another to reform it and resolve uncertainties (c.3). By a subsequent act (c.4) two more were granted to be paid by 20th October 1641. With subsidies, in general only the wealthier were taxed, half a dozen or so in villages, twenty to forty in most towns.

Poll Tax. In July 1641 by an 'Act for the speedie provision of money for disbanding the Armies and settling the peace of the two Kingdoms of England and Scotland' (16 Charles I c.9) a Poll Tax was voted. Few records of this survive. Some certificates for Lincolnshire and Staffordshire are at the House of Lords Record Office.

Contribution and Loan towards the relief of distressed Subjects in Ireland (c.30). This is discussed above.

Assessment (or Grant). This was agreed by Parliament in December 1641. The preamble to legislation for the Assessment reads:

'An Act for the raising and leavying of moneys for the necessary defence and great affairs of the Kingdoms of England and Ireland and for the payment of Debts undertaken by Parliament ... and in order to suppress that most wicked and execrable rebellion in Ireland' (16 Charles I c.32). Ironically, the administration of this Assessment was strikingly similar to that of the reviled Ship Money scheme.

The tax to some extent broke new ground. A fixed sum, £400,000, was to be raised from the whole country and this was broken down by counties in the Act (see Appendix 2, page 15). It was left to the commissioners to divide this first among the hundreds and then into parish totals. Assessors were appointed as in the subsidies to raise the parish amounts by assessments on individuals, but how this was done is not known. All Parliament did was to lay down the exemption limits, which were £1 in land, £3 in goods and £10 in wages, and then say that everyone who qualified was to pay his proportionate share. The wage limit was enough to exempt the ordinary labourer. Despite the fact that exemption limits were, apart from the wage clause, the same as those for the subsidy, the net was cast more widely, many more taxpayers were roped in and the assessments finely graded down as low as a few pence in a some cases; in some places fractions of a penny were taken into account.

Aliens and recusants had to pay double, and half of this was to be no part of the £400,000 but 'surplusage' and disposed of for the purpose of the Act; if they did not contribute under this they paid a poll tax of 2s.8d. Payment was to be made in two equal amounts, the first to be taxed before 20th May 1642 and paid into the exchequer before 20th June and the second to be taxed before 20th November 1642 and paid before 20th December.

An interesting and a most useful feature of the tax was that unlike the subsidy 'every person to be rated and taxed shall be so in every county for the estate he hath and if he have an estate in severall places in one county then to be rated in the said severall places in each severall county'. As a result of this some individuals appear as taxpayers in more than one parish and it should be possible to obtain some idea of the extent of a man's property. This rarely occurs in the subsidy and, when it does, in theory at any rate, it should be accompanied by the certificate of residence excusing him from payment in all but his home parish.

The great importance of this assessment, in comparison with other taxation records of this time, is its low tax threshold. For instance, at Banbury in Oxfordshire there were 47 subsidy taxpayers in May 1641 [P.R.O. E 179/164/481]. A year later 328 taxpayers were named in the assessment. This is doubly useful as neither Protestation nor Collection are extant. Unfortunately, such tax assessments survive only sporadically.

Other taxation records

Records of the 1641 Subsidies survive in some quantity. They have all been examined, and their condition and the very approximate number of names are noted; as have the far fewer records of the 1642 Assessment. The occasional 1641 Poll Tax records also appear.

Although heavy tax assessment continued throughout the Civil War and Commonwealth, its records are few. The occasional survivals in P.R.O. class E 179 are duly noted, particularly if they have been published.

The same goes for occasional publications relating to Ship Money or raising money to repair St. Paul's Cathedral in London, two of the rare sources which may list taxpayers or subscribers during the 1630's. Class E 179 has some records of Ship Money defaulters. Such unpublished records have not been listed here.

Conclusion

As with my other Guides, this attempts to tell researchers of records listing quantities of names. Whilst I have provided a general historical background and some detail about the records, no attempt is made to discuss their content, let alone their significance and how this might be interpreted. Much is based on T.L. Stoate's introduction to his edition of *Somerset Protestations and Lay Subsidies*; and on Cliff Webb's article in the *Genealogists' Magazine* which first gave wide publicity to the Collection. John Wilson's introduction to his edition of the Buckinghamshire Collection has also been of great use. David Cressy's *Literacy and the Social Order* has helped a great deal, both as a check on the returns with signatures and marks and also for information on other sources, in particular the Covenants, on which the section above is based. Information on the various taxes comes from Stella Colwell's *Family Roots*, which she has amplified specially for this Guide.

J.S.W.G.

Sources and Further Reading

J. Bell, *A New and Comprehensive Gazetteer of England and Wales*, 1834 (reprinted in C. Humphery-Smith, *The Phillimore Atlas and Index of Parish Registers*, 1984).

M.J. Burchall, *East Sussex contributors to the relief of Irish Protestants 1642*, Sussex Genealogical Centre, Occasional Paper No. **10**, 1984.

Stella Colwell, *Family Roots: Discovering the Past in the Public Record Office*, London, 1991, 'Later Tudor and Stuart Taxes before the Civil War', pp. 55-57.

David Cressy, *Literacy and the Social Order*, Cambridge U.P., 1980, chapter 4, 'Literacy and Loyalty', pp. 62-103, appendix pp. 191-201, notes pp. 215-21.

J.S.W. Gibson, *Oxfordshire and North Berkshire Protestation Returns and Tax Assessments 1641-42*, Oxon. Record Soc. vol. **59** and Banbury Historical Soc. vol. **24**, 1994. This includes much of the introduction to the earlier Oxon. R.S. edition of the Protestation Returns (vol. **36**, 1956) by C.S.A. Dobson.

A.J. Howard and T.L. Stoate, *The Devon Protestation Returns, 1641*, Pinner, 1973.

T. Moule, *The English Counties Delineated*, 1830 (reprinted as *The County Maps of Old England*, Studio Editions, 1990).

Public Record Office. *Exchequer K.R. Lay Subsidy Rolls, Class E 179*. List and Index Society, vols. **44** (Beds. - Essex), **54** (Glos. - Lincoln), **63** (London - Somerset), **75** (Staffs. - Yorks.), **87** (Wales, Cinque Ports, Royal Household), 1969-1973.

Royal Commission on Historical Manuscripts, *Fifth report*, Part One. Report and appendix (C.1432), H.M.S.O., 1876, pages 120-134. List of extant Protestation Returns.

T.L. Stoate, *The Cornwall Protestation Returns*, Bristol, 1974.

T.L. Stoate, *The Somerset Protestation Returns and Lay Subsidy Rolls 1641/2*, Bristol, 1975.

G.T. Warner, C.H.K. Marten and D.E. Muir, *The New Groundwork of British History*, 1943.

Cliff Webb, 'The Collection for Distressed Protestants in Ireland, 1642', *Genealogists' Magazine*, vol. **21**, no. 9, March 1985.

C.R. Webb, *The Relief of Irish Protestants Rolls: Surrey, 1642*, East Surrey FHS R.P. **25** (microfiche), and West Surrey FHS microfiche series **2**, 1988.

W.F. Webster, *Protestation Returns 1641/2 - Lincolnshire*, Nottingham, 1984.

W.F. Webster, *Protestation Returns 1641/2 - Nottinghamshire and Derbyshire*, 1980.

John Wilson, *Buckinghamshire Contributions for Ireland 1642...*, Buckinghamshire Record Society, vol. **21**, 1983. The Act of 16 Charles I c.30 is printed as an Appendix.

F.A. Youngs jr., *Guide to the Local Administrative Units of England.* Vol. **1**, *Southern England*, 1980, revised 1981; Vol. **2**, *Northern England*, 1991. Royal Historical Society.

Appendix One

The Protestation, signed by Members of the House of Commons on 3rd May 1641 and by Protestant peers the following day::

'I, A.B., do in the Presence of Almighty God, promise, vow, and protest to maintain and defend, as far as lawfully I may, with my Life, Power, and Estate, the true Reformed Protestant Religion, expressed in the doctrine of the Church of England, against all Popery and Popish Innovations, within this realm, contrary to the same Doctrine and according to the Duty of my Allegiance, His Majesty's Royal Person, Honour and Estate, as also the Power and Privileges of Parliaments, the lawful Rights and Liberties of the subjects, and every Person that maketh this Protestation, in whatsoever he shall do in the lawful pursuance of the same; and to my power, and as far as lawfully I may, I will oppose and by all good Ways and Means endeavour to bring to condign Punishment all such as shall, either by Force, Practice, Counsels, Plots, Conspiracies or otherwise, do any Thing to the contrary of any Thing in this present Protestation contained; and further that I shall, in all just and honourable ways, endeavour to preserve the Union and Peace betwixt the Three Kingdoms of England, Scotland and Ireland; and neither for Hope, Fear, nor other Respect, shall relinquish this Promise, Vow and Protestation.'

On 6th May a Bill was introduced in the House of Commons, imposing the obligation of signing the Protestation upon all Englishmen. It provided that those who refused to sign were to be held incapable of holding office, and that Peers who refused to sign were to be deprived of their seats in the House of Lords. It was doubtless this latter provision which led the Upper House to reject the Bill on 29th July. But on 30th July, the House of Commons passed a resolution that all who refused the Protestation were unfit to hold office in Church or Commonwealth, and this was ordered to be printed. It was not, however, until the following January that the Protestation itself was printed (many of the Buckinghamshire returns were written on the back of this printed letter). Copies were sent down to the sheriffs without further delay and accompanying them was a letter of instructions from the Speaker of the House of Commons:-

'Gentlemen,

It is now some months since the Protestation taken by the Lords and House of Commons was sent down into the country, with an Expectation, that it should be generally taken throughout the Kingdom, for a Testimony of their good Concurrence with the Parliament; but through the Remissness of some of those that had the Care of recommending it to others, very many there be that have not hitherto taken it; Now the House of Commons, having discovered many dangerous Designs plotted against the Parliament, and especially, that of the Fourth of this Instant January [the attempt made by King Charles in person to arrest Sir Arthur Hesilrigge, Denzil Holles, John Pym, William Strode, and John Hampden in the House of Commons], which, had it taken Effect, would have strucken not only at the Privileges, but at the very Being of Parliament (as will more appear by the Declaration herewith sent unto you, which the House desires you to publish throughout all Parts of the County) have thought fit once again to recommend the Taking of this Protestation; and have therefore commanded me, in their name, to desire you the High Sheriff and the Justices of the Peace of that County to meet together in one Place, as soon as possible you may, and there to take the Protestation yourselves; and then, dispersing yourselves into your several Divisions, that you will call together the Minister, the Constables, Churchwardens, and Overseers of the Poor of every Parish, and tender unto them Churchwardens, the Protestation, to be taken in your Presence, and to desire of them, that they will very speedily call together the Inhabitants of their several Parishes, both Householders and others, being of Eighteen Years of Age and upwards, into One or more Places, according to the Largeness of their Parishes, and to tender unto them the same Protestation, to be taken in their Presence; and to take their Names, both of those, that do take it, and do refuse to take the same Protestation; and to return them to yourselves, at such time as you shall appoint; which the House desires may be so speedily, from them, to the Knights and Burgesses serving for that County before the .... Day of ....; wherein the House desires your greatest care and Diligence, as a Matter very much importing the Good both of the King and Kingdom; which being all I have in Command, I rest,

Your very loving Friend.

London, January 19th 1641.'

Appendix Two

The Act of 16 Charles I c.32, 'for the raising and levying of Moneys for the necessary defence and great affairs of the Kingdomes of England and Ireland and for the payment of debts undertaken by the Parliament', the sum to be raised being £400,000. The quotas were as follows:

co	Bedford	£ 4,372	1s	
	Berkshire	£ 5,628	14s	2d
	Buckinghams	£ 6,712	2s	6d
	Cambridges	£ 6,199	11s	1d
	Isle of Ely	£ 2,297		
city & co	Chester	£ 326	15s	
co	Cornwall	£10,110	15s	9d
	Derbys	£ 2,819	1s	7½d
	Devon	£29,035	12s	3d
city & co	Exon	£ 1,049	4s	3d
co	Dorset	£ 7,701	2s	3d
town & co	Pool	£ 80	18s	6d
co	York	£17,380	5s	6d
city & co	York	£ 1,231	4s	9d
town & co	Kingston on H	£ 419	5s	9d
co	Essex	£18,048	9s	9d
	Glos	£ 9,978	5s	5d
city & co	Glos	£ 1,118	14s	
co	Herefords	£ 7,146	4s	6d
	Hertfords	£ 7,525	10s	
	Huntingdons	£ 3,533	8s	9d
	Kent	£20,281	15s	7½d
city & co	Canterbury	£ 818	14s	9d
co	Lancaster	£ 4,353	11s	3d
	Leicesters	£ 3,848	5s	
	Lincolns	£12,951	15s	10½d
city & co	Lincoln	£ 532	1s	9d
city of	London	£42,476	16s	3d
co	Middlesex	£12,354	12s	9d
	Monmouth	£ 1,588	6s	3d
	Northamptons	£ 4,869	16s	6d
	Nottinghams	£ 2,913	14s	3d
town & co	Nottingham	£ 96	10s	6d
co	Norfolk	£21,908	6s	1½d
city & co	Norwich	£ 2,544	4s	6d
co	Oxon	£ 6,418	4s	9d

co	Rutland	£ 1,053	14s	3d
	Shropshire	£ 4,560	5s	3d
	Staffords	£ 3,743	10s	3d
city & co	Litchfield	£ 88	7s	
co	Somerset	£16,879	13s	
city of Bristoll, same co		£ 927	4s	6d
co	Southampton	£12,464	11s	9d
town & co	Southampton	£ 513	18s	9d
	Isle of Wight	£ 1,713	4s	6d
co	Suffolk	£20,609	17s	
	Surrey	£10,808	1s	3d
	Sussex	£10,914	15s	9d
	Warwicks	£ 5,113	6s	3d
city & co	Coventry	£ 658	2s	6d
co	Worcesters	£ 5,802	10s	6d
city & co	Worcester	£ 356	4s	9d
co	Wiltshire	£11,704	19s	
	Anglesey	£ 418	18s	3d
	Brecknock	£ 850	13s	9d
	Cardigan	£ 1,008	6s	9d
	Carmarthen	£ 829	10s	9d
	Carnarvon	£ 348	8s	3d
	Denbigh	£ 447	6s	9d
	Flints	£ 274	5s	6d
	Glamorgan	£ 1,084	17s	6d
	Merioneth	£ 259	18s	3d
	Montgomery	£ 1,013	12s	6d
	Pembroke	£ 956	15s	6d
	Radnor	£ 601	19s	9d
town & co	Haverford the West	£ 83	7s	3d
co	Cumberland	£ 633	18s	
co	Durham	£ 1,309	13s	
	Westmorland	£ 547	1s	4½d
	Newcastle	£ 245	14s	
	Northumberland	£ 830	2s	4½d

The above is followed by lists of names of county commissioners. The names of Popish recusants were to be certified by the Clerks of Assize, the Peace, and ministers and churchwardens of every parish. It appears that the commissioners were to issue precepts to 2-8 'of the most substantiall discreet and honest persons Inhabitants' (s9) as appropriate for the number of inhabitants, who were 'by all convenient wayes and meanes other than by corporall oath' to enquire into the substance and value of persons to be charged and then certify their names, substance and value to the commissioners 'after the usual manner ... without respect of any former taxation heretofore had', on a penalty of £5 for refusal to act. Spiritual persons were to be rated on their temporal possessions as lay people. Any appeal lay to the commissioners.

Editorial method and cartography

The *Protestation Returns*, as sent in to Parliament, are at the House of Lords Record Office, and these have mostly been physically examined by Jeremy Gibson.

The records of the *Collection in Aid of Distressed Protestants in Ireland* are at the Public Record Office (classes SP 28 and E 179). They have all been physically examined by Cliff Webb.

Records of the *Subsidies* of 1641 and *Assessment* or *Grant* of 1642 are at the Public Record Office (class E 179), and have all been physically examined by Alan Dell. The P.R.O. class list dates these by regnal year, which sometimes suggest a Subsidy might have been in 1640. Effectively the money was raised in 1641, so this date has been given to all Subsidy records. Often the actual date of collection, normally in the preamble, has been lost. The class list does not distinguish between Subsidies and the Assessment/Grant. In the absence of clear information in the document, it has been assumed that returns with far more names than usual for a Subsidy are for the Assessment. Very approximate numbers of taxpayers are shown in round brackets against each reference. The P.R.O. E 179 reference is shown in square brackets against each document (the class reference of 'E 179' itself being omitted in all cases).

The administrative area (above the parish or township) for the taking of the Protestation, payment of taxes etc., was normally the Hundred. The nomenclature varied from county to county, with Wapentakes in the north east, Wards in the north, whilst in the south in counties with a great many small Hundreds, these were grouped in Divisions (Dorset, Hampshire), Rapes (Sussex) and Lathes (Kent). So far as possible the modern or accepted spelling for hundreds and places is used, with archaic spellings appearing in the original documents shown in square brackets, and accepted alternatives shown in round brackets. There are inevitably discrepancies and inconsistencies. The parish was not necessarily the unit of administration. Townships or hamlets may be recorded separately, or parishes grouped together. Over the centuries places changed hundred, or might (especially with enclaves) for convenience be returned under a different hundred.

Outline county maps, prepared by Jeremy Gibson, show the approximate boundaries of hundreds or other major administrative areas. This is, we believe, the first countrywide attempt to show these on easily read maps, though they exist in modern versions for various counties in volumes of the Victoria County History, the Place Names Society and other publications. Some local record offices publish them (that for Gloucestershire is particularly useful).

The initial sources have been the gazetteers of Thomas Moule (1830) and James Bell (1834), both available as reprints. The county maps show boundaries of hundreds etc., but these are indistinct and buried amongst a mass of other topographical detail. The maps in this Guide are the outcome of hours with magnifying glass and tracing from photocopies on a light table. Simplified and on small scale, they cannot show small enclaves in other hundreds (or even counties), and, without place names (impossible on this scale), these would mean little. The purpose is to give a general idea of the area of a county in which a hundred might lie. For anything more precise, gazetteers and other sources must be consulted. For this reason too, scales and the names of neighbouring counties are omitted.

The abbreviations 'm.' and 'ms.' are for membrane(s) - the parchment strips about six to nine inches wide and often stitched together to make them several feet long, sewn at the top, on which the taxation records were usually entered.

With any new Guide, especially one listing what must be tens of thousands of places, documents (and their references), some errors, misinterpretations or straightforward misprints are inevitable. Notification of corrections, alterations or additions required will be much appreciated by the editors.

BEDFORDSHIRE

Parishes: 127.

Bedfordshire continued

Protestation Returns (1)

Published: **Stodden Hd.** (and Leightonstone Hd., Hunts.), Swineshead [parish register], in *Bedfordshire Parish Registers*, **7**, p. 159, ed. F.G. Emmison, Bedford, 1933.

***Bedfordshire Record Office,** Bedford.*
Stodden Hd.: Swineshead, in parish register, published.

No Bedfordshire returns at *House of Lords Record Office*, but Swineshead is extant under Hunts.

Collection in Aid of Protestants in Ireland (55)

Public Record Office
[Redbornstoke and Wixhamtree Hds. in SP 28/191; others in E 179/243/4].

Barford Hd.: [Great] Barford, Ravensden, Renhold, Roxton, Wilden.
Flitt Hd.: Barton [in the Clay], Caddington, Clophill [Clapwell], Haynes, Higham Gobion, Luton, Pulloxhill, Shillington [Shitlington], Silsoe, Streatley.
Redbornstoke Hd.: Ampthill, Cranfield, Elstow, Flitwick, Houghton Conquest, Kempston, Lidlington, Marston Moretaine, Maulden, Milbrook, Ridgmont, Steppingley, Wilhamstead, Wotton.
Stodden Hd.: Bolnhurst, Clapham, Keysoe, Knotting, Melchbourne, Milton [Ernest], Oakley [Okely], Pertenhall, Riseley, Shelton, [Little] Staughton, Yelden; for Swineshead, *see* Hunts., Leightonstone Hd.
Wixhamtree Hd.: Blunham, Cardington, Cople, Northill, Southill, [Old] Warden, Willington.

Taxation Records

Public Record Office [E 179].

*Subsidy, **1641**:*
Bedford town (110). 2 ms [72/281]
Bedford town (80). 1 m. [72/286].
Bedford (90). One list, 1 m. [243/3].
Barford (170), **Stodden** (130), **Willey** (300) **Hds.** 3 ms. [72/280]
Manshead (250), **Flitt** (190), **Redbornstoke** (180) **Hds.** 7 ms. [72/283].
Wixhamtree (150), **Clifton** and **Biggleswade** (250) **Hds.** Poor in parts. 2 ms. [72/285].
Wixhamtree (100), **Clifton** (200), **Biggleswade** (200) **Hds.** 2 ms. [72/282].
Wixhamtree, **Clifton**, **Biggleswade Hds.** (50). Very poor. 2 ms. [72/288].

Bedfordshire continued

See also 'The ship-money papers of Henry Chester and Sir Will. Boteler, **1637-1639**', F.G. and Margaret Emmison, *Bedfordshire Historical Record Society*, **18** (1936), Assessments, lists of arrears.

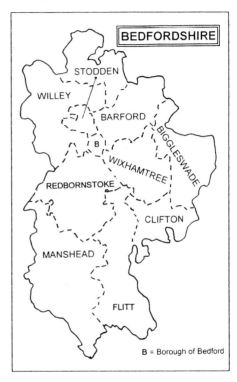

BEDFORDSHIRE

STODDEN
WILLEY
BARFORD
B
WIXHAMTREE
REDBORNSTOKE
BIGGLESWADE
CLIFTON
MANSHEAD
FLITT

B = Borough of Bedford

BERKSHIRE

Parishes: 162.

Berkshire: *Protestation Returns* continued

Protestation Returns (101)

Returns are extant for the divisions covering the centre of the county, north to south. Hundreds on the east and west are missing.

Places duplicated in the *Collection in Aid of Distressed Protestants in Ireland* are asterisked (*). Places in *italics* have names of clergy and officials only. Fifteen places have signatures and marks (mostly Abingdon Division), shown by a dagger (†). Women (§) are named in West Shefford only.

Published: Oxfordshire and North Berkshire Protestation Returns and Tax Assessments 1641-1642 (indexed), ed. J. Gibson, Oxfordshire Record Society 59 and Banbury Historical Society 24, 1994, covers the following:

Abingdon Division
Abingdon Division, clergy and officials.
Hormer Hd.: Abingdon (no *Protestation*, but a small part in Assessment, see below); †Besselsleigh, *Brightwell*, Cumnor and hamlets (incl. North and South Hinksey, Wootton), Grandpont (Cumnor), Kennington (Radley), †Radley, Shippon (Abingdon), †Sunningwell, Thrupp (Radley), Wytham.
Note. For Hormer Hd., the 1642 tax assessments (see below) are also published in this volume, together with a small part of Abingdon.
Moreton Hd.: †Ashampstead, Aston Tirrold, Aston Upthorpe (Blewbury), †Basildon, Didcot, East and West Hagbourne, Harwell, North and South Moreton, Moulsford (Cholsey), †Streatley, Upton (Blewbury).
Ock Hd.: Appleford (Sutton Courtenay), †Appleton with Eaton, Drayton, *Frilford (Marcham), *Fyfield, Garford (Marcham), *Goosey (Stanford in the Vale), Kingston Bagpuize, *Lyford (Hanney), *Marcham, †Milton, †Steventon, Sutton Courtenay, †Little Wittenham, †Long Wittenham.

House of Lords Record Office.

Abingdon Division
Hormer, Moreton, Ock Hds. *Published*, as above.

Newbury Division
Newbury Division, clergy and officials.
Compton Hd.: Aldworth, Chilton, Compton, Farnborough, East and West Ilsley.
Faircross Hd.: Beedon, Boxford, Brightwalton, Brimpton, Chieveley (incl. Courage Snelsmore and Oare), Frilsham, Greenham (in Thatcham), Hampstead Norris, Leckhampstead, Midgham, *Newbury, Peasemore, Shaw cum Donnington, Speenhamland, Stanford Dingley, Wasing, Welford, Winterbourne [Danvers], Woodspeen and Bagnor, Yattendon.

Newbury Division continued
Kintbury Eagle Hd.: Avington (wrongly identified as Abingdon, so listed and filed under Abingdon Division), Chaddleworth, East and West Challow, Enborne, Fawley, Hampstead Marshall, Hungerford, Inkpen, Kintbury, Letcombe Bassett and Regis, Shalbourn, †Little (East) Shefford, §West Shefford, Speen Church, *West Woodhay*.

Reading Division
Reading Hd.: †Beenham, Blewbury, †Bucklebury, Cholsey, Pangbourne, **Reading** (St. Giles, St. Lawrence, St. Mary), Sulhamstead Abbots, Thatcham, Tilehurst.
Sonning Hd.: Sonning [Sunninge towne in Sunning Hd.].
Theale Hd.: Aldermaston, Bradfield, Burghfield, Englefield [Inglefield], †Padworth, *Purley*, *Shinfield, Sulham, Sulhamstead Bannister, *Tidmarsh*, Ufton [Nervet], Woolhampton.

Berkshire Record Office, Reading, has photocopies of all Berkshire returns. An indexed transcript is held by John Townsend, see right.

Collection in Aid of Protestants in Ireland (49)

Places duplicated in the *Protestation Returns* are asterisked. An indexed transcript is held by John Townsend, see right.

Public Record Office
[All in SP 28/191 except Lyford, in E 179/272/44].

Beynhurst Hd.: Shottesbrook, White Waltham.
Bray Hd.: Bray.
Charlton Hd.: Barkham, Finchampstead, [Broad] Hinton, *Shinfield, *Sonning (incl. Earley); Swallowfield.
Faircross Hd.: *Newbury.
Faringdon Hd.: *for* Faringdon *see* Shrivenham Hd.
Ganfield Hd.: Buckland, Charney Bassett, Hatford, Longworth, Pusey, Shellingford.
Lambourn Hd.: Lambourn.
Moreton Hd.: East Garston.
Ock Hd.: *Appleton, *Frilford, *Fyfield, Goosey, *Kingston Bagpuize, *Lyford [E 179/272/44], *Marcham, Stanford in the Vale.
Ripplesmere Hd.: Easthampstead, Winkfield.
Shrivenham Hd.: Ashbury, Baulking, Bourton, Buscot, Coleshill, Compton Beauchamp, Eaton Hastings, Great Faringdon (Wadley, Littleworth and Thrupp in), Fernham (in Shrivenham) [Feaunhamforth], Longcott, Shrivenham (parish) incl. Watchfield Liberty; Uffington.
Sonning Hd.: Arborfield, Hurst; *for* Sonning, *see* Charlton Hd.
Theale Hd.: *for* *Shinfield *see* Charlton Hd.
Wantage Hd.: Ardington, Fawler (in Sparsholt), East and West Hendred, Kingston Lisle (in Sparsholt), East Locking.

Berkshire: *Collection* continued

An indexed transcript of both *Protestation Returns* and the *Collection in Aid of Distressed Protestants in Ireland* is held by John Townsend, 95 Arbor Lane, Winnersh, Wokingham, Berks. RG11 5JE. Searches by arrangement. Fee payable.

Taxation Records

Published: Assessment, 164? for **Hormer Hd**, in *Oxon and North Berkshire ... Tax Assessments 1641-42*, as above.

Public Record Office [E 179].

Subsidy, 1641:
County (120). Poor and fading. 1 m. [75/352].
Cookham (70), **Bray** (60), Wargrave (80), Beynhurst (40), **Ripplesmere** (50), Charlton (130), **Sonning** (100) **Hds**. 6 ms. [75/356].
Cookham (70), **Bray** (50), Wargrave (70), Ripplesmere (90), Charlton (60), **Sonning** (50), Beynhurst (40) **Hds**. 4 ms. [75/362].
Faringdon (180), Ganfield (90), Lambourn (50), Shrivenham (150), **Wantage** (150) **Hds.** Mostly poor. Hds only, individual places not indicated. 7 ms. [75/360].

Berkshire: *Subsidy* continued

Faringdon (100), **Ganfield** (100), **Lambourn** (60), **Shrivenham** (200), **Wantage** (170) **Hds**. Poor in parts. 10 ms. [75/358].
Lambourn Hd. (35). Fragment. 1m. [75/354].
Hormer (30), **Ock** (140), **Moreton** (140) **Hds**. Gaps. 7 ms. [75/353].
Hormer (130), **Ock** (170), **Moreton** (140) **Hds**. 7 ms. [75/357].
Reading Hd. and **Borough** (200). **Theale Hd**. (150). 9 ms. [75/355].
Wantage and **Shrivenham Hds**. (200). Poor. 4 ms. [75/361].
New Windsor (140). Includes burgesses. 3 ms. [75/359].

Assessment, 1642:
Hormer Hd. (300): Abingdon (mostly missing, a small part only), Besselsleigh, Cumnor and hamlets (incl. North and South Hinksey, Wootton), Grandpont (Cumnor), Kennington (Radley), Radley, Shippon (Abingdon), Sunningwell, Wytham. 4 ms. [75/376]. *Published,* as above.

Relief of Ireland, 1641:
Beynhurst, Wantage Hds.: 10 ms. (400+) [243/20]. Somewhat muddled. Each parish separate.

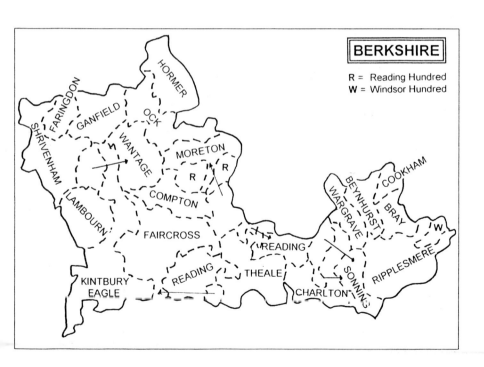

BUCKINGHAMSHIRE

Parishes: 206.

| Protestation Returns (57) |

Returns at the House of Lords Record Office are extant only for the two northern hundreds of Buckingham and Cottesloe; places duplicated in the *Collection in Aid of Distressed Protestants in Ireland* are asterisked (*).

Women are named (§) in eight places: Addington, Adstock, Lillingstone Dayrell, Twyford, Aston Abbots and Drayton Parslow, and in family groups at Little Horwood and Winslow (mostly 'and his wife'). There are signatures and marks (†) at Foxcott, Lillingstone Dayrell, Thornborough and Little Horwood.

Places naming clergy and officials only in *italics*.

Most returns are on the back of the printed protestation issued to parishes.

In the published edition of the *Collection* (see right), for ten places the tax lists are so specifically doubling as *Protestation Returns* (for which there are none extant at the House of Lords R.O.) that it would be inappropriate to omit mention.

Published: Caversfield (Buckinghamshire enclave in Oxfordshire) in *Oxfordshire and North Berkshire Protestation Returns and Tax Assessments 1641-42,* ed. J. Gibson, Oxfordshire Record Society 59 and Banbury Historical Society 24, 1994.

In *Buckinghamshire Contributions for Ireland 1642...,* John Wilson, Buckinghamshire Record Society 21 (1983):

Ashendon Hd.: Ashendon with Pollicott, Aston Sandford, Long Crendon, Ickford, Worminghall.

Newport Hd.: Great Linford, Loughton, Newton Longville, Shenley Church End, Stoke Hammond.

House of Lords Record Office.

Buckingham Hd.: *§Addington, *§Adstock, Akeley, Barton (Hartshorn), *Beachampton, Biddlesden, Caversfield *(published),* Chetwode, Edgcott, †Foxcott, Hillesden, *Leckhampstead, *†§Lillingstone Dayrell, Marsh Gibbon, *(Maids) Moreton, *Padbury, Preston Bissett, Radclive cum Chackmore, Shalstone, Steeple Claydon, Stowe, *†Thornborough, *Thornton, Tingewick, Turweston, §Twyford, Water Stratford, Westbury.

Cottesloe Hd.: *§Aston Abbots, *Cheddington, Cholesbury [two copies], *Cublington, *§Drayton Beauchamp and *Parslow, *Dunton, *Edlesborough, Grove, *Hardwick and *Weedon, *Hoggeston, *Great Horwood, *§†Little Horwood [two copies], *Ivinghoe, *Linslade, *Marsworth cum Hawridge, *Mentmore, *Mursley,* *Pitstone cum Nettleden, *Slapton, *Soulbury, *Stewkley, *Swanbourne, *Tattenhoe,* *Whaddon cum *Nash, *Whitchurch, *Wing, *Wingrave, *§Winslow; *Cottesloe Hd.,* clergy and officials.

Public Record Office [SP 28/191].

Places as published, above.

Buckinghamshire continued

| Collection in Aid of Protestants in Ireland (132) |

Places duplicated in the *Protestation Returns* (or with these attached) are asterisked.

Published: Buckinghamshire Contributions for Ireland 1642..., John Wilson, Bucks. Record Soc. 21, 1983, from P.R.O. SP 28/149, SP 28/191 and E 179/244/6. About 8,000 names. Indexed.

Ashendon Hd.: *Ashendon with Pollicott, *Aston Sandford, Brill, Chilton with Easington, East Claydon with Botolph Claydon, Middle Claydon, *Long Crendon, Grendon Underwood, *Ickford, Kingsey, North Marston, Oving, Towersey, Waddesdon, Lower Winchendon, *Worminghall.

Aylesbury Hd.: Aston Clinton and St. Leonard, Aylesbury with Walton, Bierton with Broughton, Bledlow, Buckland, Cuddington, Dinton, Ellesborough, Haddenham, Halton, Great Hampden, Hartwell with Little Hampden, Horsenden, Hulcott, Great and Little Kimble, Great and Little Missenden, Monks Risborough, Princes Risborough, Stoke Mandeville, Stone, Wendover, Weston Turville (with Lee).

Buckingham Hd.: *Addington, *Adstock, *Beachampton, *Leckhampstead, *Lillingstone Dayrell, *Maids Moreton, *Padbury, *Thornborough, *Thornton.

Burnham (Chiltern) Hd.: Chalfont St. Giles, Farnham Royal.

Cottesloe Hd.: *Aston Abbots, *Cheddington, *Cublington, *Drayton Beauchamp and *Parslow, *Dunton, *Edlesborough, *Hardwick with *Weedon, *Hoggeston, *Great and *Little Horwood, *Ivinghoe, *Linslade, *Marsworth, *Mentmore, Mursley, *Nash, *Pitstone, Shenley Brook End, *Slapton, *Soulbury, *Stewkley, *Swanbourne, *Whaddon, *Whitchurch, *Wing, Wingrave, *Winslow with Shipton.

Newport Hd.: Astwood, Bletchley (incl. Eaton and Stratford), Bradwell, Cold Brayfield, Bow Brickhill, Great and Little Brickhill, Calverton, Chicheley, Clifton Reynes, North Crawley, Emberton, Hanslope, Hardmead, Haversham, Lathbury, Lavendon, *Great Linford, Little Linford, *Loughton, Milton Keynes, Moulsoe, Newport Pagnell, *Newton Longville, Olney with Warrington, Ravenstone, *Shenley Church End, Sherington, Simpson, Stantonbury, Stoke Goldington, *Stoke Hammond, Stony Stratford West and East, Tyringham with Filgrave, Walton, Wavendon, Weston Underwood, Willen, Wolverton, Great Woolstone, Woughton on the Green.

Stoke (Chiltern) Hd.: Colnbrook, Horton.

Public Record Office

[mostly in SP 28/191; some in E 179/244/6; SP 28/149 is a duplicate, the accounts of the sheriff, Richard Grenville, which has been the primary source for the published version].

Records as published, above.

Buckinghamshire continued

NEWPORT

BUCKINGHAM

COTTESLOE

ASHENDON

AYLESBURY

BURNHAM

DESBOROUGH

STOKE

BUCKINGHAMSHIRE

Taxation Records

Published: Assessment, **1642**, Boycott, Lillingstone Lovell (Oxfordshire enclaves in Buckinghamshire) [P.R.O. E 179/164/496A], in *Oxon ... Tax Assessments 1641-42*, ed. J. Gibson, Oxon. R.S. **59** and Banbury H.S. **24**, 1994, as left.

Public Record Office [E 179].

Subsidy, 1641:
Aylesbury 3 Hds. (500). 4 ms. [80/302].
Aylesbury 3 Hds. (500). 4 ms. [80/308].
Wendover (20), Brandsfee (20); a few gaps. 2 ms. [244/5].
Buckingham 3 Hds. (220). 2 ms. [80/305].
Buckingham 3 Hds. (170); poor in places. 3 ms. [00/306].
Buckingham (50). 1 m. [80/297].
Borough of Buckingham with Bourton (50). 1 m. [80/301].
Chiltern 3 Hds. (Burnham, Desborough, Stoke) (700); faded. 5 ms. [80/298].
Cottesloe 3 Hds. (350). 2 ms. [80/299].
Cottesloe 3 Hds. (300). 5 ms. [80/300].

Buckinghamshire: *Subsidy* continued

Cottesloe 3 Hds. (300); poor in places. 5 ms. [80/303].
Newport 3 Hds. (500); faded. 7 ms. [80/296].
Newport 3 Hds. (500); very faded. 4 ms. [80/314].
Newport 3 Hds. (750); fading. 4 ms. [80/307].

Poll Tax/Assessment, 1641:
Cottesloe 3 Hds.: account. (300+). 10ff. [244/3].
Parish of Waddesdon (250). Paper, 8 ff. [244/4].

Relief of Army in Ireland, 1645(?):
Newport Pagnell ('Towne of Newport Pagnel, Tichford End, North End, Marsh End') (350); in poor condition, not examined in detail. 8 ms. [244/7].

Assessment (for garrison of Aylesbury), 1644-46:
Iver (incl. Thorney) (90). 4 ms. [244/8].

See also *Ship Money Papers and Richard Grenville's Note-Book*, ed. C.G. Bonsey and J.G. Jenkins, Buckinghamshire Record Society, **13**, 1965. Lists of those in arrears in the county, **1635**. Indexed.

CAMBRIDGESHIRE

Parishes: 171.

Protestation Returns

House of Lords Record Office.

Returns survive only for the University, none for the county. They are much fuller and more interesting than those for Oxford University. Full names are given for those in residence (surnames only for those absent), degrees etc shown at Corpus Christi and Emanuel (Oxford has surnames only throughout). Names of 'privileged tradesmen' also given (not at Oxford).

Cambridge University: Christ's College, Clare Hall, Corpus Christi College, Emanuel College, Gonville and Caius College, Jesus College, King's College, Magdalene College, Pembroke Hall, St. John's College, St. Katherine's Hall, St. Peter's College, Sidney Sussex College, Trinity College, Trinity Hall; persons having the privilege of scholars; public officers.

Collection in Aid of Protestants in Ireland

Public Record Office [SP 28/191].

Papworth Hd.: Conington (only).

Cambridgeshire continued

Taxation Records

Public Record Office [E 179].

Subsidy, 1641:
Cambridge by wards (150). 1m. [83/397].
Cambridge by wards (230). 1m. [83/409].
Cambridge. Too poor condition to be examined. 1 m. [83/419].
Armingford (150), **Longstow** (150) **Hds.** 3 ms. [83/403].
Armingford (200), **Longstow** (200) **Hds.** 3 ms. [83/411].
Chilford (100), **Radfield** (60), **Whittlesford** (70) **Hds.** 4 ms. [237/12].
Chilford (120), **Radfield** (120), **Whittlesford** (30) **Hds.** 3 ms. [83/399].
Chilford (90), **Radfield** (100), **Whittlesford** (65) **Hds.** 3 ms. [83/404].
Papworth (250), and **Northstow** (200) **Hds.** 2 ms. [83/402].
Papworth (150), **Chesterton** (90), **Northstow** (100) **Hds.** 2 ms. [83/408].
Papworth (130), **Chesterton** (80), **Northstow** (75) **Hds.** 2 ms. [83/418].
Papworth (150), **Chesterton** (120), **Northstow** (100) **Hds.** 4 ms. [83/413].

Cambridgeshire: *Subsidy 1641* continued

Staploe (120); **Staine** (80), poor; **Flendish** (60); **Cheveley** (50) **Hds.** 2 ms. [83/400].
Staploe (100), **Staine** (70), **Flendish** (60), **Cheveley** (40) **Hds.** faded in places, 4 ms. [83/405].
Staploe (100), **Staine** (80), **Flendish** (60), **Cheveley** (40) **Hds.** 6 ms. [83/417].
Wetherley (150), **Thriplow** (100) **Hds.** 2ms. [83/407].
Wetherley (150), **Thriplow** (120) **Hds.** 14 ms. [83/410].
Isle of Ely (600). 4 ms. [83/398].
Isle of Ely (est. 400). Holes in places. 4 ms. [83/406].
Ely (100) and **(North and South) Witchford** (100) **Hds.** 2 ms. [83/414a].
Wisbech (150) and **North Witchford** (60) **Hds.** 2 ms. [83/414].

Assessment, 1642:
Cambridge. University (30).
Mayor and Burgesses (15).
By parishes: All Saints (50), Holy Sepulchre (25), St. Andrew the Great (60), St. Andrew the Less (25), St. Benedict (40), St. Botolph (20), St. Clement (40), St. Edward (40), St. Giles (30), St. Mary the Great (80), St. Mary the Less (25), St. Michael (20), St. Peter (15). 5 ms. [83/401].
Wetherley (420), **Thriplow** (270) **Hds.** 3 ms. [83/412].
Whittlesford Hd. (300). 3 ms. [83/420].
Isle of Ely (est. 600); faded. 4 ms. [83/421].

Scots Loan:
1645. County. Account. 28 ms. [244/18].
1646. County. Account. 60 ms. [244/19].
These two items are really account books, entitled 'The account of Peter Collins/Collyns of Cambridge of several sums of money collected by him in the (towne and) county of Cambridge' They give names, locations and amounts. No attempt has been made to estimate numbers as there must be repetition.

Account of Levies, 1647:
Longstow Hd. Account of levies (300); difficult and fading badly. 1 m. [83/425].
Thriplow Hd. Account of levies (170); badly mutilated and fading. 2 ms. [83/426].

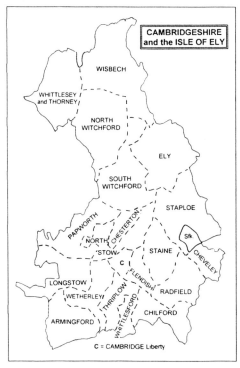

CAMBRIDGESHIRE and the ISLE OF ELY

WISBECH
WHITTLESEY and THORNEY
NORTH WITCHFORD
ELY
SOUTH WITCHFORD
STAPLOE
Sfk
PAPWORTH
NORTH
CHESTERTON
'STOW
STAINE
CHEVELEY
C
FLENDISH
LONGSTOW
WETHERLEY
THRIPLOW
RADFIELD
WHITTLESFORD
CHILFORD
ARMINGFORD

C = CAMBRIDGE Liberty

CHESHIRE

Parishes: 130.

Protestation Returns (8)

Published: Lymm, 'A brief account of the Lymm Protestation of 1641', M. Jackson, *North Cheshire FHS* **14**(1), 1987, pp. 7-11, 145 names.

House of Lords Record Office.

The returns for Chester appear to be all of signatures (or marks) except for St. Peter's parish. There are no extant returns for the county.

Chester (city): Holy Trinity, St. Bridget, St. Martin, St. Mary on the Hill, St. Michael, St. Olave, St. Oswald [part filed under 'Lincs'], St. Peter.

Remonstrance, 1641

British Library Manuscripts Collection.
[Harleian Ms. 2107]

Loose Papers bound up together: 'The names of all the Inhabitants within the County of Chester'. The catalogue entry concludes 'All these Subscriptions abovementioned do not include near the Number of the then substantial Inhabitants of the County-Palatine of Chester'. Approx. 8,400 names.

There appear to be 84 separate returns, in no coherent order, including 26 unidentified, one 'subscribed by many of principall Gentry (1642)', being 48 in number' and another with 'the names of the Justices of the Peace, & of the Jury, at the Quarter-Sessions'. Those places that are named are here listed by hundred. The catalogue entry gives the number of Subscribers in each return.

This return is briefly discussed by David Cressy, *Literacy and the Social Order*, 1980, page 71.

Broxton Hd.: (Gt.) Boughton, Christleton, Crewe, Eccleston, Plemstall, Pulford.
Bucklow Hd.: Baguley (Bowdon), Bexton (Knutsford), Bollington (Bowdon), Bowdon [Bodon] (2), Carrington, Knutsford (Rostherne), Lymm [Lyme], Mobberley, Peover [Peever], Ringway [Ringey in Bowdon], Rostherne [Rousthorne].

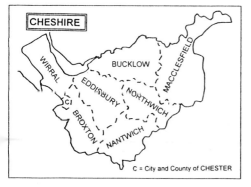

C = City and County of CHESTER

Cheshire: *Remonstrance* continued

Chester: Chester Castle and the Gloverstone.
Eddisbury Hd.: Acton, Barrow, Gt and Lit Budworth, Bunbury, Edleston (Acton), Over (2), Seven Oaks (Gt. Budworth), Tarporley [Torporley], Tarvin [Turvyn], Thornton (le Moors), Weaverham.
Macclesfield Hd.: Alderley (2), Chelford, Macclesfield, Siddington, Stockport, Wilmslow [Wineslowe], Withington.
Nantwich Hd.: Audlem [Ardren], Baddiley [Baddeley], Barthomley, Burland (Acton), Cholmondeston, Haslington (Barthomley), Nantwich, Poole, Sandbach, Wybunbury [Wibunbury] (2).
Northwich Hd.: Davenham, Middlewich, Northwich (2), Peover - see Bucklow Hd., Sandbach, Warmingham [Warmingcham].
Wirral Hd.: Bidston, West Kirby [Kirkeby], Neston, Shotwick, Stanney, Woodchurch.

Collection in Aid of Protestants in Ireland (2)

Public Record Office [SP 28/191].

Bucklow Hd.: Dunham (Massey), High Legh (only).

Solemn League and Covenant, 1646 (?)

Published: Woodchurch, 'The Solemn League and Covenant in Wirral', *Wirral N&Q*, **1** (1892), p. 58. Stated to be 1646, but more probably 1643.

Taxation Records

Public Record Office [E 179].

Subsidy, 1641:
Broxton (150), **Nantwich** (150) **Hds.**; only a few names per parish. 3 ms. [85/135].
Broxton Hd. (200); only a few names per parish. 2 ms. [85/131].
Macclesfield Hd. (170); only a few names per parish. 2 ms. [85/136]
Macclesfield Hd. (130); only a few names per parish. 2 ms. [85/137].
Wirrall and **Eddisbury Hds.** (50), 1 m. [85/134].

Chester City Record Office, Chester.

Poll Tax, 1641:
Chester: Eastgate Ward [CAS/1].

Subsidy, 1641-2:
Chester (roll) [CAS/2/11].
Chester (papers) [CAS/2/12].

See also 'Loans, contributions, subsidies, and ship money, paid by the **clergy of the diocese of Chester**, in the years ... **1634, 1635, 1636,** and **1639...**', ed. G.T.O. Bridgeman, in *Miscellanies relating to Lancashire and Cheshire*, vol. **1**, 1885. Transcripts. The contributions of 1634-6 were for the repair of St. Paul's Cathedral, London.

CORNWALL

Parishes: 204.

> **Protestation Returns (167)**

Published: The Cornwall Protestation Returns, ed. T.L. Stoate. Bristol, 1974. 30,653 names. Surname index. The county is complete except for Jacobstow, St. Austell, Truro and St. Neot. Women (§) are named in St. Mabyn and St. Tudy. Family groups are shown in Crantock and Newlyn. Lists of clergy and officials collated with parish returns. Cornwall has far more returns with signatures or marks than any other county, indicated here by a dagger (†).

East Hd.: †Anthony [Jacob], Botus Fleming, †Callington, †Calstock, †Egloskerry, †Landrake (incl. St. Erney), Landulph, Laneast, Launceston, Lawhitton, Lewannick, Lezant, †Linkinhorne, †Maker, †Menheniot, Northill, South Petherwin, Pillaton, Quethiock, Rame, †St. Dominick, †St. Germans (parish and borough), St. Ive, †St. John, St. Mellion, St. Stephen's by Launceston, St. Stephen's by Saltash, †St. Thomas by Launceston, †Sheviock, †South-hill, Stoke Climsland, †Tremaine, †Tresmeer, Trewen; East Hd., clergy and officials.

Kerrier Hd.: Breage [Breock], †Budock, †Constantine, Cury, †Germoe, †Grade, †Gunwalloe, †Gwennap, †Helston, †Landewednack, †Mabe, †Manaccan, Mawgan in Meneage, †Mawnan, †Mullion, †Mylor, †Penryn and St. Gluvias, †Perranarworthal, †Ruan Major and †Minor, †St. Anthony in Meneage, St. Keverne, †St. Martin in Meneage, †Sithney, †Stithians [Stedians], †Wendron; Kerrier and Penwith Hds., clergy and officials.

Lesnewth Hd.: †Advent, †Altarnun [Altarnum], †Camelford borough (misfiled under East Hd.), †Davidstow, †Forrabury, †Lanteglos, †Lesnewth (parish), †Michaelstow, †Minster, †Otterham, Poundstock, †St. Clether, †St. Gennys, †St. Juliot, †Tintagel, †Treneglos, †Trevalga, †Warbstow; Lesnewth Hd., clergy and officials.

Penwith Hd.: †Camborne, †Crowan, †Gulval, Gwinear, †Gwithian, †Illogan, Ludgvan, †Madron, †Marazion or Market Jew, †Morvah, †Paul, †Penzance, Perranuthnoe, †Phillack, †Redruth [St. Uny], †St. Buryan, St. Erth, †St. Hilary, †St. Ives, †St. Just in Penwith, †St. Levan, †Sancreed, Sennen, †Towednack, †Uny Lelant, †Zennor; Penwith Hd.: clergy and officials - see Kerrier Hd.

Cornwall: Protestation Returns continued

Powder Hd.: †Cornelly, †Creed, Cuby, Fowey, †Gerrans, †Gorran, †Grampound, Kea, Kenwyn, Ladock, †Lamorran, †Lanlivery, †Lostwithiel, †Luxulian [Luscullian], †Merther, †Mevagissey, †Philleigh, †Probus, Roche, †Ruan Lanithorne, †St. Allen, †St. Anthony in Roseland, †St. Blazey, †St. Clement, †St. Dennis, †St. Erme, †St. Ewe [Eva], †St. Feock, †St. Just in Roseland, †St. Mewan, †St. Michael Caerhays, †St. Michael Penkevil, †St. Sampson, †St. Stephen in Brannel, †Tywardreath, †Veryan; Powder Hd., clergy and officials (incl. St. Austell).

Pyder Hd.: Colan, Crantock, Cubert, †Lanhydrock, Lanivet, Mawgan, Newlyn, Padstow, Perranzabuloe, Little Petherick, St. Agnes, St. Breock, St. Columb Major and Minor, St. Enoder, St. Ervan, St. Eval, St. Issey, St. Merryn, St. Wenn, Withiel; Pyder Hd., clergy and officials.

Stratton Hd.: †Boyton, †Bridgerule, †Kilkhampton, †Launcells, †Marhamchurch, †Morwenstow, †North Tamerton, †Poughill, †Stratton (parish), †Week St. Mary, †Whitstone; Stratton Hd., clergy and officials.

Trigg Hd.: †Blisland, Bodmin, Egloshayle, †Helland, †St. Breward, †St. Endellion, †St. Kew, †§St. Mabyn, †St. Minver [Mynfrey], †St. Teath, †§St. Tudy; Trigg Hd., clergy and officials.

West Hd.: Boconnoc, Braddock [Broadoak], †Cardinham, Duloe, †East Looe borough and †St. Martin's parish, Lanreath, Lansallos, Lanteglos by Fowey, †Liskeard, Morval, Pelynt, St. Cleer, †St. Keyne, †St. Pinnock, St. Veep, St. Winnow, Talland and West Looe, Warleggan.

House of Lords Record Office.

Returns as published, above.

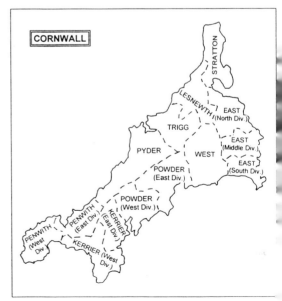

Collection in Aid of Protestants in Ireland (1)

Public Record Office [SP 28/191].

Powder Hd.: St. Dennis (only).

Taxation Records

Public Record Office [E 179].

Subsidy, 1641:
East Hd. (southern division) (330). 2 ms. [89/329].
Penwith (400), Kerrier (350) Hds. 6 ms. [89/325].
Penwith and Kerrier Hds. (1,000+). 6 ms. [89/330].
Penwith Hd. (?1642 assessment) Not examined, too fragile. 2 ms. [89/342].
Pyder (500), Powder (600) Hds. 7 ms. [89/324].
Powder Hd. (900); bad in parts. 5 ms. [89/339].
Pyder Hd. (550). 3 ms. [89/327].
Pyder Hd. (750); gaps. 5 ms. [89/331].
Pyder Hd. (200); fading badly. 1 m. [89/333].
Pyder Hd. (300); very bad. 2 ms. [89/341].
Stratton Hd. (300). 1 m. [89/335].
Trigg and Lesnewth Hds.? (est. 400); poor. 6 ms. [89/328].
Trigg (250), Lesnewth (300) Hds. 6 ms. [89/334].
Trigg Hd.(200); poor. 3 ms. [89/337].
West Hd. (est. 500); damaged and fading. 3 ms. [89/326].

Assessment, 1642:
Trigg Hd. (1,200); last page fading. 8 ms. [89/338].
West Hd. (1,800); excellent condition. 8 ms. [89/340].

Cornwall Record Office, Truro

Transcript of Lay Subsidies at P.R.O., c.1591-1667, for **Talland** parish only.

CUMBERLAND

Parishes: 144.

Protestation Returns (106)

Most of the county is covered. No less than nineteen places, all in Allerton-above-Derwent Ward, as indicated by §, mention women, though often un-named ('and his wife', 'et uxor'). Greystoke is the only place with signatures and marks (†). Addingham, uniquely, gives ages.
Places naming clergy and officials only in *italics*.

Published: 'Caldbeck in 1642', *Cumberland and Westmorland Archaeological Society, Transactions*, N.S. **21**, 1921, pp. 276-79.

House of Lords Record Office.

Allerdale-above-Derwent Ward: Arlecdon (parish), §Beckermet St. Bridget, §Bootle, Brigham, §Chapel Sucken [family groups], §Cleator, Cockermouth, §Corney, Dean, Distington, §Egremont, Embleton, *Ennerdale*, §Eskdale [Eshdale], Gosforth, Haile, §Harrington [widows], *Irton*, Lamplugh, Lorton, Loweswater, §Millom, Moresby, §Muncaster, §Ponsonby [family groups], §St. Bees (incl. §Wasdale and §Wasdalehead) [family groups, very good], §Thwaites, §Ulpha, §Waberthwaite, §Whicham, §Whitbeck, Workington; *Allerdale Ward*, clergy and officials.

Allerdale-below-Derwent Ward: Allhallows, Aspatria, Bassenthwaite, Bolton, Bridekirk, Bromfield (incl. Langrigg, Mealrigg, Crookdale, Scales [Staple?], Allonby, (West) Newton, 'Kelsicke', Dundraw, 'Whaprigg', Blencogo), Caldbeck *[published]*, Camerton, Crosscanonby, Crosthwaite (Thornthwaite, St. John Castlerigg [Castrige?], Braithwaite, Coledale, Borrowdale, Keswick, Under Skiddaw), Dearham, Gilcrux, Holme Cultram, Ireby, Isel (and townships), Plumbland, Torpenhow, Uldale, Westward.

Cumberland Ward: Aikton, Beaumont, Bowness (-on-Solway), Burgh-by-Sands, **Carlisle** St. Cuthbert and St. Mary, Dalston, Grinsdale, Kirkandrews(-on-Eden), Kirkbampton, Kirkbride, Orton, Sebergham, Thursby, Warwick, Wetheral, Wigton; *Cumberland Ward*, clergy and officials.

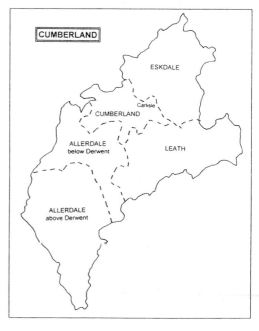

CUMBERLAND

ESKDALE

Carlisle

CUMBERLAND

ALLERDALE below Derwent

LEATH

ALLERDALE above Derwent

Cumberland: *Protestation Returns* continued

Eskdale Ward: Arthuret, Bewcastle, Brampton, Castle Carrock, Crosby-on-Eden, Cumrew, Cumwhitton, Nether and Upper Denton, Farlam, Hayton, Irthington, Kirkandrews(-on-Esk), Kirklinton, Lanercost, Scaleby, Stanwix, Stapleton, Walton.

Leath Ward: Addingham (incl. Maughamby, Glassonby, Unthank, Gamblesby, Farmonby and Roberby, Hunsonby and Winskill, Little Salkeld) [gives ages], Ainstable, Castle Sowerby, Croglin, Dacre (incl. Soulby, Wray, Stainton, Newbiggin, (Gt.) Blencow, Threlkeld), †Greystoke [Graystock] (incl. Water Millock, Grisedale, Motherby and Gill, Hutton-Soil and Penruddock, Hutton-Roof, Berrier, Johnby, (Little) Blencow), Hesket-in-the-Forest, Hutton-in-the-Forest, Kirkland (incl. Culgaith), Kirkoswald, Langwathby, Lazonby, Melmerby, Newton [Reigny], Ousby, Penrith, Renwick, Great Salkeld, Skelton.

Cumbria Record Office, Carlisle.
Photostats of original returns; transcripts (two, ms and ts) and index (ms).

Cumbria Record Office, Barrow-in-Furness.
Microfilm of original returns.

Note. Taxes raised at this time tended to be at least partially in aid of the northern counties of England, so it is not surprising that there are no records of money raised either from the *Aid to Distressed Protestants in Ireland* or from the *Subsidy* of 1641, which were presumably not levied in these counties.

DERBYSHIRE

Parishes: 172.

Protestation Returns

Published: *Nottinghamshire and Derbyshire Protestation Returns 1641-2*, transcribed and published by W.F. Webster, Mapperley, Nottingham, 1980, this covers:
Kedleston, Pentrich and South Wingfield, from parish registers.
Kedleston. *Phillimore's Derbyshire Marriages*, vol. **13**, pp. 184-85.
Pentrich. As above, vol. **14**, pp. 235-39.
South Wingfield. As above, vol. **14**, pp. 229-233.
The parish register lists for these three places show signatures and marks.

Derbyshire: *Protestation Returns* continued

Derbyshire Record Office, Matlock.
Kedleston, Pentrich, South Wingfield, in parish registers, *published*, as above.
Ashover, in parish register [D253 A/PI 1/1].
Elton [D258 M/60/6].
Staveley, in parish register [D661 A/PI 1/1].

No returns at *House of Lords Record Office.*

Taxation Records

Public Record Office [E 179].

Subsidy, **1641***:*
Derby borough (50). 1 m. [93/367].
Derby borough (50). 1 m. [94/372].
Morleston and Litchurch Wapentake (150). 3 ms. [93/368].
Repton and Gresley Wapentakes (150). 3 ms. [93/366].
Morleston and Litchurch (200), **Wirksworth** (150), **Repton and Gresley** (120), **Appletree** (250) **Wapentakes.** 13 ms. [94/371].

Assessment, **1642***:*
High Peak Wapentake(400); paper in parts. 5 ms. [94/373].
Scarsdale Wapentake (600). 8 ms. [245/5].

There are no records of the *Collection in Aid of Distressed Protestants in Ireland.*

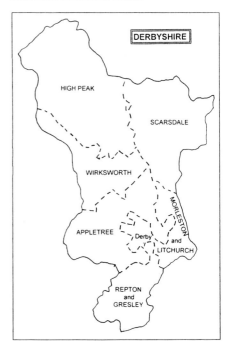

DEVON

Parishes: 468.

Devon: *Protestation Returns* continued

Protestation Returns (412)

The whole county is extant apart from the Hundreds of Axminster, East Budleigh and Ottery St. Mary. A few places (38) with signatures and marks are indicated by a dagger (†). No returns mention women

Published: *The Devon Protestation Returns, 1641*, ed. A.J. Howard ... and T.L. Stoate. 2 vols., Pinner, the editor, 1973. Indexed. Names within each place arranged alphabetically. 63,000 names. Lists of clergy and officials collated with parish returns.

Axminster Hd.: Axmouth, transcript from parish register.

Bampton Hd.: †Bampton (parish) (Patton and Shillingford), Burlescombe (later in Halberth Hd.), Clayhanger, †Hockworthy, †Holcombe Rogus, †Morebath, Uffculme; *Bampton, Halberton, Hayridge, Hemyock and Tiverton Hds.*, clergy and officials.

Black Torrington Hd. - see under Torrington

Braunton Hd.: Ashford, Barnstaple, Berrynarbor, Bratton Fleming, Braunton (parish), East and West Buckland, Combe Martin, East and West Down, Filleigh, Georgeham, Goodleigh, Heanton Punchardon, Ilfracombe, Kentisbury, Marwood, Morthoe, Pilton, Trentishoe.

West Budleigh Hd.: Cheriton Fitzpaine, Poughill, †Shobrooke, Stockleigh English, Stockleigh Pomeroy, †Upton Helions, Washfield.

Cliston Hd.: Broadclyst, Butterleigh.

Coleridge Hd. (North Div.): †Ashprington, †Blackawton, †Cornworthy, Dartmouth (St. Clement, St. Patricks [Petrox], St. Saviour), Dittisham, †Halwell, †Harberton, †Stoke Fleming, †Totnes; *Coleridge (North Div.) Hd.*, clergy and officials.

Coleridge Hd. (South Div.): Buckland Tout Saints, Charleton, Chivelstone, Dodbrooke, Southpool, East Portlemouth, Sherford, Slapton, Stokenham; *Coleridge (South Div.) Hd.*, clergy and officials.

Colyton Hd.: Colyton (parish).

Crediton Hd.: †Colebrook, Crediton, †Kennerleigh, †Morchard Bishop, Newton St. Cyres, Sandford.

Ermington Hd.: Aveton Gifford, Bigbury, Cornwood, Ermington (parish), Harford, Holbeton, Modbury, Newton Ferrers, Ringmore, Ugborough; *Ermington and Plympton Hds.*, clergy and officials.

Exeter (borough): Exeter (Allhallows Goldsmith Street, Allhallows on Walls, Heavitree, Holy Trinity, St. David, St. Edmund [upon the Bridge], St. George [the Martyr], St. John [Bowe], St. Kerrian, St. Lawrence, St. Leonard, St. Martin, St. Mary Arches, St. Mary Major, St. Mary Steps, St. Olave, St. Pancras, St. Paul,

Exeter continued: St. Peter [Cathedral], St. Petrox [Petrock], St. Sidwell, St. Stephen,); *Exeter (all parishes)*, clergy and officials. See also article detailed on page 28.

Exminster Hd.: Ashcombe, †Ashton, Bishopsteignton, Chudleigh, Dawlish, Doddiscombsleigh, Dunchideock, Exminster (parish), Ide, Kenn, Kenton, Mamhead, Powderham, †Chillingford St. George, East and West Teignmouth, Trusham; *Exminster Hd.*, clergy and officials.

Fremington Hd.: †Alverdiscott, †Fremington (parish), Horwood, Huntshaw, Instow, Newton Tracey, Roborough, St. Giles [in the Wood], Tawstock, Great Torrington, Westleigh.

Halberton Hd.: Halberton (parish and tithings), Sampford Peverell, Willand; *Halberton Hd.*, clergy and officials - see Bampton Hd.

Hartland Hd.: Clovelly, Hartland (parish), Welcombe, Woolfardisworthy, Yarnscombe; *Hartland Hd.*, clergy and officials - see with Black Torrington Hd.

Hayridge Hd.: Bickleigh, Bradninch, Broadhembury, Cadbury, Cadeleigh, Cullompton, Feniton, Kentisbeare, Nether Exe, Payhembury, Plymtree, Shildon, Silverton, Talaton, Thorverton; *Hayridge Hd.*, clergy and officials - see Bampton Hd.

Haytor Hd.: Abbotskerswell, Berry Pomeroy, Brixham, Broadhempston, Buckland-in-the-Moor, Churston Ferrers, Cockington, Coffinswell, Denbury, Haccombe, Little Hempston, Ipplepen, Kingskerswell, Kingswear, Marldon, Marychurch, Newton Abbot and Wolborough, Paignton, Staverton, Stoke Gabriel, Torbryan, Tormoham, Widecombe-in-the-Moor, Woodland; *Haytor and Teignbridge Hds.*, clergy and officials.

Hemyock Hd.: Awlescombe, Buckerell, †Churchstanton, Clayhidon, Culmstock, Dunkeswell, Hemyock (parish); *Hemyock Hd.*, clergy and officials - see Bampton Hd.

Lifton Hd.: Bradstone, Bratton Clovelly, Bridestowe, Broadwoodwidger, Dunterton, Germansweek, Kelly, Lamerton, Lewtrenchard, Lifton (parish), Lydford, Marystow, Marytavy [Tavy St. Mary], Okehampton, Sourton, Stowford, Sydenham Damarell, Thrushelton, Virginstow.

South Molton Hd.: East and West Anstey, Chittlehampton, Knowstone, Landkey, Molland, North Molton, South Molton (town and parish), Nympton St. George, Satterleigh, Swimbridge, Bishops Tawton, Twitchen, Warkleigh; *South Molton Hd.*, clergy and officials - see with North Tawton Hd.

Plympton Hd.: Plympton St. Mary and St. Maurice, Plymstock, Revelstoke, Shaugh Prior, Wembury, Yealmpton; *Plympton Hd.*, clergy and officials, see Ermington Hd.

Roborough Hd.: Bere Ferrers, †Bickleigh, Egg Buckland, Buckland Monachorum, Meavy, Plymouth, Petertavy [St. Peter Tavy], Sampford Spiney, Sheepstor [Shittestor], Stoke Damarell, Tamerton Foliot, Walkhampton, Whitchurch.

Shebbear Hd.: Abbotsham, Alwington, Beaford, Bideford, Buckland Brewer, Buckland Filleigh, Bulkworthy, Frithelstock, Huish, Iddesleigh, Lancross, Langtree, Littleham, Meeth, Merton [Martin], Monkleigh, Newton St. Petrock, Northam, Parkham, Peters Marland, Petrockstow, East Putford, Shebbear (parish), Sheepwash, Little Torrington, Wear Giffard; *Shebbear Hd.*, clergy and officials - see with Black Torrington Hd.

Shirwell Hd.: Arlington, Highbury, Brendon, Challacombe [Raleigh], Charles, Countisbury, †Loxhore, Lynton, Martinhoe, Parracombe, Shirwell (parish), Stoke Rivers.

Stanborough Hd. (North Div.): †Brent South, Dartington, †Diptford, †North Huish, †Moreleigh, Rattery; *Stanborough (North Div.) Hd.:* clergy and officials.

Stanborough Hd. (South Div.): East Allington, West Alvington, Churchstow, South Huish, Kingsbridge, Loddiswell, Malborough, South Milton, Thurleston, Woodleigh; *Stanborough (South Div.) Hd.*, clergy and officials.

Stanborough Hd.: Buckfastleigh, Dean Prior, †Holne (filed separately).

Tavistock Hd.: †Brent Tor, Milton Abbot, Tavistock (parish).

North Tawton and Winkleigh Hd.: Ashreigney; Atherington; High Bickington [Bickerton]; Bondleigh; Burrington; Clanaborough; Dolton; Dowland; Down St. Mary; Lapford with Chawleigh, Coldridge, Brushford, Wembworthy and Eggesford; Broad Nymet; Nymet Rowland and Tracy; North Tawton; Winkleigh (parish); Zeal Monachorum; *North Tawton, South Molton and Witheridge Hds.*,clergy and officials; *Winkleigh Hd.*, clergy and officials - see with Black Torrington Hd.

Teignbridge Hd.: Bickington, North Bovey, [South] Bovey Tracy, Hennock, Highweek, Ideford, Ilsington, Kingsteignton, Lustleigh, Manaton, Moretonhampstead, Teigngrace; *Teignbridge Hd.*, clergy and officials - see with Haytor Hd.

Tiverton Hd.: †Calverleigh, †Hunsham, †Loxbeare, Tiverton (parish), Uplowman; *Tiverton Hd.*, clergy and officials - see Bampton Hd.

Black Torrington Hd.: Abbots Bickington, Ashbury, Ashwater, Beaworthy, Belstone, Bradford, Bradworthy, Bridgerule, Broadwoodkelly, Clawton, Cookbury, Exbourne, Halwill, Hatherleigh, High-ampton, Hollacombe, Holsworthy, Honeychurch, Inwardleigh, Jacobstowe, Luffincott, Milton Damerel, North Lew, Monkokehampton, Pancrasweek, North Petherwin, Pyworthy, St. Giles in the Heath, Sampford Courtenay, Sutcombe, Tetcott, Thornbury, Black Torrington (parish), Werrington,

Black Torrington Hd. continued: West Putford; *Black Torrington, Hartland, Shebbear and Winkleigh Hds.*, clergy and officials.

Winkleigh Hd. - see North Tawton Hd.

Witheridge Hd.: Cheldon, Chulmleigh, Creacombe, Cruwys Morchard, Mariansleigh [Marleight], Meashaw, Bishops Nympton, Kings Nympton, Oakford, Puddington, Rackenford, Romansleigh, Rose Ash, Stoodleigh, Templeton, Thelbridge, Washford Pyne, Witheridge (parish), Woolfardisworthy, East and West Worlington; *Witheridge Hd.*, clergy and officials - see with North Tawton Hd.

Wonford Hd.: Alphington, Brampford Speke, †Bridford, Chagford, †Cheriton Bishop, †Christow, Combeinteignhead, Drewsteignton, †Dunsford, Exeter - *listed separately*, Gidleigh, Heavitree - *see Exeter*, †Hittisleigh, †Holcombe Burnell, Huxham, East and West Ogwell, Pinhoe, Poltimore, Rewe, St. Nicholas, Sowton, Spreyton, Stoke Canon, Stokeinteignhead, †South Tawton, Tedburn [St. Mary], †Throwleigh, Topsham, Upton Pyne, †Whitstone; *Wonford Hd.*, clergy & officials.

A detailed discussion of these returns in relation to St. Mary Arches and St. John, Exeter, is given in 'The population of two Exeter parishes in 1641-2', T.J. Falla and M.M. Rowe, *Devon & Cornwall Notes & Queries*, **35** (3), 1983, pp. 89-95.

Uffculme (Bampton Hd.), oath roll in parish chest, also published in *Devon & Cornwall Notes & Queries*, **10** (1918-19), pp. 253-56.

House of Lords Record Office.

Returns as published, above.

Devon Record Office, *Exeter*.

Bampton Hd.: Uffculme (in parish records), *published*, as above.

Taxation Records

Publication: *Devon Taxes 1581-1660*, ed. T.L. Stoate. Almondesbury, the editor, 1988. Indexed. Includes 1581 subsidy, assessments of 1642, 1647 and 1660, and poll tax of 1660. Hundreds and places covered by the **1642 assessment** [P.R.O. E 179/102/498]:

Black Torrington Hd. (all parishes; 2,125 names): Ashbury, Ashwater, Beaworthy, Belstone Kigbeare [Keckbear] (Okehampton), Abbots Bickington [Bickhampton], Bradford, Bradworthy, Bridgerule, Broadwood Kelly, Clawton, Cookbury, Exbourne, Halwill, Hatherleigh, Highampton, Hollacombe, Holsworthy, Honeychurch, Inwardleigh, Jacobstow, Luffincott, Milton Damerel, Northcott, Northlew, Monk Okehampton, Pancrasweek, North Petherwin, West Putford, Pyworthy [Pinworthie], St. Giles on the Heath, Sampford Courtenay, Sutcombe, Tetcott, Thornbury, Black Torrington (parish), Werrington.

Shebbear Hd. (missing Buckland Filleigh, Huish and Meeth; 1,333 names + c.300 illegible): Abbotsham, Alwington, Beaford, Bideford, Buckland Brewer, Bulkworthy, Frithelstock [Frethelstocke], Iddesleigh, Landcross [Lancrosse], Langtree, Littleham, Merton, Monckleigh, Newton St. Petrock, Northam, Parkham, Peters Marland, Petrockstow, East Putford, Shebbere (parish), Sheepwash, Little Torrington, Weare Gifford.

Winkleigh Hd. (149 names): Coldridge [Coulrudge], Lapford (Loosebeare).

Hartland Hd. (all parishes; 222 legible names): Clovelly (illegible), Hartland, Welcombe, Woolfardisworthy, Yarnscombe.

Hundreds and places covered by the **1647 assessment:**

Ermington Hd. [E 179 102/503] (all parishes): Aveton Gifford, Bigbury, Cornwood, Ermington (parish), Harford [Herford], Holbeton [Holberton], Kingston, Modbury, Newton Ferrers, Ringmore, Ugborough.

Plympton Hd. [E 179 102/503] (all parishes): Brixton, Plymstock, Plympton St. Mary and St. Maurice, Revelstoke, Shaugh (Prior), Wembury [Wenbury], Yealmpton.

Coleridge Hd. South Division [E 179/245/14/1]: Buckland Tout Saints, Charleton, Chivelstone, Dodbrooke, South Pool, East Portlemouth, Sherford, Slapton, Stokenham.

Coleridge Hd. North Division [E 179/102/529]: Ashprington, Blackawton, Cornworthy, Dartmouth, Dittisham, Halwell [Halwill], Harberton, Totnes (mostly missing), Townstall (Dartmouth St. Clements).

Stanborough Hd. South Division [E 179/245/14/1]: East Allington, Churchstow [Churstow], South Huish, Kingsbridge, Loddiswell, Malborough, (South) Milton, Thurlestone [Thurelstone], Woodleigh.

Stanborough Hd. North Division [E 179/102/558]:, South Brent, Buckfastleigh, Dartington, Dean Prior, Diptford, Holne, North Huish, Moreleigh, Rattery (lost).

Tavistock Hd. [E 179/102/559] (complete): Brentor, Milton Abbot, Tavistock.

Haytor Hd. [E 179/102/560] (missing Abbots-kerswell, Brixham, Kingswear, Marldon, Staverton, Torbryan, Wolborough, Buckland in the Moor): Berry Pomeroy, Broadhempston, Churston Ferrers, Cockington, Coffinswell, Denbury, Little Hempston, Ipplepen, Kingskerswell, Paignton, St. Mary Church, Stoke Gabriel, Tormoham, Widecombe in the Moor, Woodland.

See also 'Records of the Dean and Chapter of Exeter, 1633, no. 2478', O.M. Moger, *Devon & Cornwall Notes & Queries*, **26** (1954-5), pp. 124-8, and **27** (1956-8), p. 23. List of men thought fit to lend money to the Crown in Devon.

Public Record Office [E 179].

Four subsidies in two payments, 1641:
Exeter city by parishes (500), 1st and 2nd payments. 3 ms. [102/485].
Bampton (est. 200); **Hayridge** (est. 200), very faded; **Hemyock** (est. 200), **Tiverton** (200), **Halberton** (100) **Hds.** 1st and 2nd payments. 7 ms. [102/487].

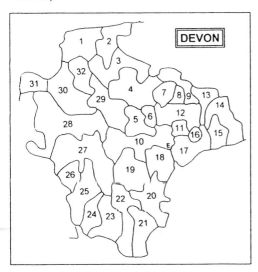

Key to Map of Devon Hundreds	
14 Axminster	20 Haytor
9 Bampton	13 Hemyock
28 Black Torrington	27 Lifton
1 Braunton	3 South Molton
17 East Budleigh	16 Ottery St. Mary
6 West Budleigh	24 Plympton
11 Cliston	25 Roborough
21 Coleridge	30 Shebbear
15 Colyton	2 Shirwell
5 Crediton	22 Stanborough
23 Ermington	26 Tavistock
E Exeter	29 North Tawton
18 Exminster	and Winkleigh
32 Fremington	19 Teignbridge
8 Halberton	7 Tiverton
31 Hartland	4 Witheridge
12 Hayridge	10 Wonford

Bampton (250), Hayridge, (1000), Hemyock (150), Tiverton (150), Halberton (150) **Hds**. 3rd and 4th payments. 6 ms. [102/497].

Coleridge (est. 1,000), bad; **Haytor** (est. 400); **Wonford South** (120); **Stanborough** (400) **Hds**., 3rd and 4th payments, poor. 16 ms. [102/492].

Fremington, Shirwell, Braunton (est. 750) **Hds**., 1st and 2nd payments; very poor. 8 ms. [102/484].

South Molton (450), Witheridge (500), **North Tawton** (400) **Hds**. 3rd and 4th payments; some faded. 10 ms. [102/488].

Plympton (400), Ermington (400) **Hds**. 3rd and 4th payments. 7 ms. [102/494].

Roborough (400), Tavistock (170), **Lifton** (300) **Hds**., 1st and 2nd payments. 10 ms. [102/486].

Roborough (300), bad in places; **Tavistock** (300); **Lifton** (350) **Hds**., bad; 3rd and 4th payments. 6 ms. [102/493].

Two subsidies in one payment, 1641:

Exeter city by wards (450). 3 ms. [245/12].

Bampton (400); **Hayridge** (600), some poor; **Hemyock** (250); **Tiverton** (250) **Hds**., some poor. 8 ms. [102/496].

Braunton (50) **Hd**., poor. [102/544].

East Budleigh (150), Ottery St. Mary (60) **Hds**, poor. 3 ms. [102/470].

West Budleigh, Teignbridge, Wonford, Exminster (400-500) **Hds**.; difficult to identify and incomplete. 9 ms. [102/513].

Cliston **Hd**. (50), very poor. 1 m. [102/514].

Colyton and Axminster (350) **Hds**., bad in parts and crumbling. 5.ms. [102/478].

Hartland and Black Torrington (1,000), **Shebbear** (200), bad; **Winkleigh** (150) **Hds**.; poor; difficult. 17 ms. [102/500].

1640/1. of Shirwell **Hd**. (50), fragment only. 1 m. [102/499].

Assessments, 1642 and 1647:

1642. Hartland (222+), Black Torrington (2,125), Shebbear (1,333+), Winkleigh (149) **Hds**.; bad gaps. 25 ms. [102/498]. *Published.*

1647. Coleridge, Ermington, Haytor, Plympton, Stanborough and Tavistock **Hds**.: *Published.* Details including document refs. above.

Assessments(?), 1655, 1657:

Two rolls: Ermington **Hd**. (400), **Plympton Hd**. (250), by parish; **Lifton Hd**. (250), **Roborough Hd**. (300), **Tavistock Hd**. (150). Lands and goods listed separately [245/11].

Somerset Record Office, Taunton.

1641. Hayridge **Hd**.: Payhembury. Persons over 16, by household, liable to tax [DD/WO 53/1].

Note. There are no records of the *Collection in Aid of Distressed Protestants* in Ireland.

DORSET

Parishes: 260.

Protestation Returns (239)

Fairly complete for the whole county, excluding the boroughs of Dorchester, Bridport and Lyme. Places asterisked also have returns for the *Collection in Aid of Distressed Protestants*, but these have *not* been published.

There are signatures and marks (†) for Bryanston, Winterborne Strickland, Warmwell, Radipole, Upwey, West Knighton, Whitcombe, Stratton and Grimston, and Todber; and some signatures for Wareham Ladychurch, Winfrith, and Charmouth. No returns mention women.

Published: Dorset Protestation Returns preserved in the House of Lords, 1641 to 1642, ed. E.A. and G.S. Fry. Place index only. *Dorset Records,* **12** [Aberdeen], 1912.

Index of names in the Dorset Protestation Returns 1641-2, B.W. Fagan, Dorset Records, **2**, 1912, reprinted Charmouth, 1960.

Blandford (North and South Divisions)

Bere Regis **Hd**.: *Bere Regis, Winterborne Kingston.

Bindon Liberty: Bindon (liberty) (*for* Chaldon Herring *see* Winfrith Hd.), *Wool. *Collection only:* *West Lulworth

Coomb's Ditch **Hd**.: Anderson, Blandford [Forum], Blandford St. Mary, Bloxworth, Winterborne Clenston, Winterborne Whitechurch.

Corfe Castle **Hd**.: Corfe Castle (borough).

Dewlish **Hd**. *see* Dorchester Div., Puddletown Hd.

Hasilor **Hd**.: Arne, *Church Knowle, *East Holme, Kimmeridge, *Steeple, *Tyneham [Tineham]. *Collection only:* *Sanwich in Purbeck.

Hundredsbarrow **Hd**.: Affpuddle, *Turnerspuddle.

Owermoigne Liberty: Owermoigne.

Pimperne **Hd**.: †Bryanston, Durweston, Fifehead [Neville], Hammoon, Hazelbury-Bryan, Langton Long Blandford, Pimperne (parish), [Iwerne] Steepleton [Preston], Stourpaine, Tarrant Hinton, Tarrant Keynston, Tarrant Launceston, Winterborne Houghton, †Winterborne Strickland.

Rowberrow **Hd**.: Langton Matravers, *Studland, Swanage, *Worth Matravers.

Rushmore **Hd**.: *Winterborne [Zelston].

Winfrith **Hd**.: Chaldon Herring, *Combe Keynes, *East Lulworth (West Lulworth - *see* Bindon Liberty), Moreton, Poxwell, *East Stoke, Wareham (Borough, Holy Trinity, St. Martin's, Ladychurch), *†Warmwell, Winfrith [Newburgh] (parish), Woodsford.

Bridport Division

Clergy and officials.

Beaminster **Hd**.: Beaminster (parish), Chardstock, Cheddington, Corscombe, Netherbury, Stoke Abbott [Abbas], Wambrook.

Beaminster Forum and Redhone Hd.: Bradpole, Mapperton, Mostertone with South Perrot.

Broadwindsor Liberty: *Broadwindsor [*Collection in* SP 28/195].

Eggerton Hd.: Askerswell, Long Bredy and Kingston, Hooke, Winterbourne Abbas, Wraxall.

Frampton Liberty: Bettiscombe, Bincombe, Burton [Bradstock], Compton Valence, Frampton (parish), Herringstone, Winterborne [Came].

Godderthorne Hd.: Allington, Shipton George, Walditch.

Loders and Bothenhampton Liberty: Bothenhampton, Loders.

Powerstock Hd.: *Powerstock [Poorstock].

Whitchurch Canonicorum Hd.: *Burstock, Charmouth, Chideock, *Marshwood, Pilsdon, Stockland, *Symondsbury [*Collection in* E 179/245/22a], Whitechurch Canonicorum (parish), *Wootton Fitzpaine.

Dorchester Division
Clergy and officials.

Culliford Tree Hd.: (*for* Broadmayne *see* George Hd.), [*Broadway], [Buckla]nd Ripers, [West] Chickerell, †West Knighton, *[Mel]combe Regis], *Osmington, †Radipole [Rodipole], West Stafford and Froome Billet, †Upwey, Weymouth, †Whitcombe, [Winterbourne Monkton]; *Collection only:* *Goven in Chickerell.

Fordington Liberty: Dallwood, Fordington, *Hermitage [*Coll.* in SP 28/195].

George Hd.: Bradford [Peverell] and Muckleford, *Broadmayne, Charminster, Stinsford, †Stratton and Grimston, Winterborne St. Martin.

Piddlehinton Liberty: Piddlehinton.

Isle of Portland Liberty: Portland.

Puddletown [Piddletown] **Hd.:** Athelhampton, Burleston and *Dewlish (North Blandford Div.), *Milborne St. Andrew, [*Puddletown], Tincleton, Tolpuddle.

Sutton Poyntz Liberty: Preston and Sutton Poyntz (2), Stockwood.

Tollerford Hd.: *East Chelborough, *West Chelborough and Luccombe, Chilfrome, 'Frome Vauchurch, *Maiden Newton, *Toller Porcorum. *Collection only:* *Evershot*, Frome St. Quintin, *Rampisham, *Toller Fratrum, *Wynford Eagle.

Uggscombe Hd.: *Abbotsbury [mis-filed under Surrey, and published separately as 'Abbotsbury Protestation Oath Return', Hector Carter, *N.Q.S. & D.*, 28, 1968, pp. 59-61]; Chilcombe, Fleet, Hawkchurch, Langton Herring, [Littlebredy], [Litton Cheney], Portesham, [Puncknowle], Swyre (*for* Weymouth *see* Culliford Tree Hd.), Winterbourne Steepleton; see also Liberties of Fordington and Piddlehinton; *Collection only:* *Ugglecorn?

Weymouth and Melcombe Regis Borough *see* Culliford Tree Hd.

Wyke Regis and Elwell Liberty: Wyke Regis.

Shaston Division
Alcester Liberty: Shaftesbury St. James.

Badbury Hd.: Chalbury, Moor Crichel, *Gussage St. Michael, *Hinton Martell, Hinton Parva [Stanbridge], Horton, Shapwick, Tarrant or Little Crawford, *Wimborne Minster and hamlets.

Cogdean Hd.: Canford Magna, Charlton Marshall, Corfe Mullen, Hamworthy, *Kinson, *Lytchett Matravers, *Lytchett Minster, Sturminster Marshall.

Cranborne Hd.: *Ashmore, Bellchalwell, Cranborne (parish, incl. Boveridge), *Edmondsham, *Farnham, *Hampreston, Holwell (in Somerset, but parsonage house in Dorset), Okeford Shilling with Keysworth, West Parley, *Pentridge, Tarrant Gunville, Tarrant Rushton Turnworth, Witchampton.

Note. There are over fifty hundreds and liberties in Dorset, many of them comprising only very few parishes or even just one. For administrative purposes these areas were grouped in Divisions, as shown on this map. There are no definitive maps showing boundaries of hundreds or their grouping in divisions, so this is based on an amalgam of nineteenth century gazetteers, the maps in the Place Names Society volumes (covering only half the county) and the *Phillimore Atlas of Parish Registers.*

DORSET

STURMINSTER Division

SHERBORNE Division

CERNE Sub-Division

Blandford

SHASTON Division

BRIDPORT Division

Poole

Wareham

DORCHESTER Division

BLANDFORD Division

Dorset: *Protestation Returns, Shaston Div.*, ctd

Gillingham Liberty: Gillingham, Bourton tithing, *Motcombe.

Knowlton Hd.: *Long Crichel, *Gussage All Saints (Gussage St. Michael - *see* Badbury Hd.), Woodlands. *Collection only:* 'Knolton'.

Loosebarrow Hd.: *Almer [*Coll.* in E 179/245/22A], Morden, Spetisbury.

Monkton Up Wimborne Hd.: Chettle, Shaftesbury [borough], St. Peter and Holy Trinity, Tarrant Monkton; *see also* Alcester Liberty.

Sixpenny Handley [Hadley or Hanley] **Hd.:** Cann [Shaston St. Rumbold] (Melbury tithing), *Compton Abbas, Fontmell Magna, [Sixpenny] Handley, Iwerne Minster, Melbury Abbas.

Wimborne St. Giles Hd.: *Wimborne All Saints (Wimborne Minster *see* Badbury Hd.), *Wimborne St. Giles.

Sherborne Division (with Cerne and Sturminster)
Clergy and officials (also for *Cerne Sub-Division* and *Sturminster Division*).

Halstock Liberty: Halstock.

Ryme Intrinseca Liberty: Ryme Intrinseca.

Sherborne Hd.: Beer Hacket [Hackwood], Bradford Abbas, Castleton, Bishops Caundle, *Purse Caundle, Caundle Marsh, Up Cerne, Nether and Over Compton, Folke, Haydon, Holnest, Lillington [Shinborne], Longburton, Lydlinch, Oborne, *Sherborne (town), Thornford, North Wootton.

Yetminster Hd.: Batcombe, Chetnole, Leigh, Melbury Bubb, Melbury Osmond, Yetminster (parish).

Cerne Sub-Division
Clergy and officials - *see* Sherborne Divison.

Alton Pancras Liberty: Alton Pancras.

Buckland Newton Hd.: *Buckland Newton (parish) and tithings, *Mappowder, *Plush, Pulham, *Glanvilles Wootton.

Cerne, Totcombe and Modbury Hd.: *Cattistock, Cerne Abbas, Nether Cerne, Compton Abbas *or* West Compton, Godmanston.

Piddletrenthide Liberty: *Minterne Magna, *Piddletrenthide.

Sydling Liberty: *Broadsidling and Hilefield, Sydling [St. Nicholas].

Whiteway Hd.: Cheselbourne, Hinton [Helton], *Ibberton, *Melcombe Horsey (and Bingham), *Milton Abbas, Stoke Wake, Wolland.

Sturminster Division
Clergy and officials - *see* Sherborne Divison.

Brownshall Hd.: Stourton Caundle, Stalbridge, Stock Gayland.

Redland Hd.: Buckhorn Weston, *Fifehead Magdalen, *Iwerne Courtney [Shroton] and Farringdon, Kington Magna, *Manston [*Coll.* in SP 28/195], Childe Okeford, Silton, East *and* West Stour, Sutton Waldron, †Todber.

Stour Provost Liberty: Stour Provost.

Dorset: *Protestation Returns, Sturminster Div.* ctd.

Sturminster Newton [Castle] Hd.: *Hinton St. Mary, Margaret Marsh, *Marnhull, *Okeford Fitzpaine, *Sturminster Newton [Castle] (parish, incl. Newton and Woodland, Bagber).

Brief extracts (clergy signatories only) from the Protestation Returns are also given in 'Dorset Clergy and the Protestation of 1641-2', *Notes and Queries for Somerset and Dorset*, **4**, 1894-5, pp. 223-26, 260-64, 313-16.

House of Lords Record Office.

Returns as published, above.

Collection in Aid of Protestants in Ireland (88)

Places for which returns exist are asterisked in the above list of Protestation Returns. Unless otherwise stated they are in SP 28/191. There are two unidentified places, one in SP 28/191 and one in E179/245/22A. In addition, there are returns for the following places, as yet unidentified:

Buckland Ludred, Childerford, Knolton, Ugglecorn, Westpilly.

Taxation Records

Public Record Office [E 179].

Subsidy, 1641-2:
Blandford Division (500). 3 ms. [105/329].
Bridport Division (600). 5 ms. [105/328].
Dorchester Division: Dorchester Borough (60), **Weymouth and Melcombe Regis Borough** (60), **Culliford Tree Hd.** (60), **Puddletown Hd.** (80), **Uggscombe Hd.** (140), **[St.] George** (80), remaining Liberties (100). 5 ms. [105/331].
Poole (40). 1 m. [105/332].
Poole (40), poor. 1 m. [105/333].
Shaston Division (400). 5 ms. [105/335].
Shaston Division (100), **Badbury Hd.** (700), **Sixpenny Hadley Hd.** (600), **Monkton-up-Wimborne Hd.** (200); **Gillingham Liberty** (200). 15 ms. [105/336].
Sherborne Division (1,000). 6 ms. [105/330].

Poll Tax, 1641:
Boroughs of **Blandford** (45) and **Wareham** (35), Hds. of **Winfrith** (120), **Pimperne** (180), **Rushmore** (25), **Hundredsbarrow** (100), **Bere Regis** (70), Liberties of **Bindon** (65), **Dewlish** (30), **Owermoigne** (15) [105/334].

See also 'Ship-money [1635]: Longbedy, Dorset', A.W. Vivian-Neal, *N.Q.S.D.*, **20** (1930-32), pp. 234-35. List of taxpayers.

Co. DURHAM

Protestation Returns (80)

The complete county is covered except for Staindrop. No returns have signatures and marks. No returns mention women.

Published: Durham protestations, or the returns made to the House of Commons in 1641-2 for the maintenance of the protestant religion for the county palatine of Durham ..., ed. H.M. Wood. Surtees Society, vol. **135**, 1922. Indexed.

Chester Ward: Boldon, Chester-le-Street and townships, Ebchester, Edmondbyers, Esh, Gateshead [Gateside], Hunstonworth, Jarrow, Lamesley, Lanchester, Medomsley, Monkwearmouth, Muggleswick, Ryton, South Shields [St. Hilda], Tanfield, Washington, Whickham, Whitburn, Witton Gilbert; *Chester Ward*, clergy and officials.

Darlington Ward: Auckland St. Andrew and townships, Auckland St. Helen, Aycliffe, Barnard Castle, Brancepeth, Cockfield, Coniscliffe, Darlington (parish), Denton, Gainford, Hamsterley, Haughton [le Skerne], Heighington, Merrington, Middleton-in-Teasdale, Sadberge, Stanhope, Whitworth, Whorlton, Winston, Witton le Wear, Wolsingham; *Darlington Ward*, clergy and officials.

Easington Ward: Bishop Wearmouth, Castle Eden, Croxdale, Dalton-le-Dale;

Durham: St. Mary le Bow North Bailey, St. Mary South Bailey, St. Giles, St. Margaret, St. Nicholas; Easington (parish), Houghton-le-Spring, Kelloe, Monk Hesledon [Hesleton], Pittington, St. Oswald, Seaham, Sherburn House [Hospital], Sunderland, Trimdon.

Stockton Ward: Billingham, Bishop Middleham, Bishopton, [Low] Dinsdale, Eaglescliffe, Elton, Elwick [Hall], Greatham, Grindon, Hart, Hartlepool, Hurworth, Middleton St. George, Long Newton, Norton with Stockton, Redmarshall, Sedgefield, Sockburn, Great Stainton, Stranton.

Note. For Berwick upon Tweed, technically in co. Durham, see under Northumberland.

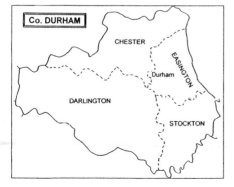

House of Lords Record Office.

Returns as published, left.

Durham County Record Office, Durham.

Easington Ward: Easington (parish), Monk Hesledon, in parish registers, with signatures and marks.

Note. Taxes raised at this time tended to be at least partially in aid of the northern counties of England, so it is not surprising that there are no records of money raised either from the *Aid to Distressed Protestants in Ireland* or from the *Subsidy* of 1641-42, which were presumably not levied in these counties.

ESSEX

Parishes: 405.

Sixteen Essex parishes have lists with signatures and marks, indicated by a dagger (†), all except Middleton in parish registers. These have been analysed in detail (but without names) by David Cressy in *Literacy and the Social Order: Reading and Writing in Tudor and Stuart England*, Cambridge University Press, 1980, pp. 77-96.

Protestation Returns (43)

Apart from occasional parish register entries, returns are extant only for the northern Hinkford Hundred. Amongst these women (§) are listed at Belchamp St. Paul, and a few are mentioned at Ashen and Felstead.

Published: **Becontree Hd.:** Wanstead, 'The Wanstead protestation 1641', *East Anglian Miscellany* **1922**, p. 81.

Dunmow Hd.: Barnston, *Manchester Genealogist,* Autumn 1969, p. 18; *Essex Review*, vol. **25**, pp. 55-64; *Ecclesiastical History of Essex*, by H.D. Smith, pp. 94-95, Colchester, n.d.

Chelmsford Hd.: Boreham, *Manchester Genealogist*, Winter 1970, pp. 11-12.

Chafford Hd.: Childerditch, *Essex Review*, **26**, 93.

Dengie Hd.: Dengie, *Essex Review*, **32**, 34-35.

House of Lords Record Office.

Hinckford Hd.: Alphamstone, §Ashen, Ballingdon, Belchamp Otton, §Belchamp St. Paul, Belchamp Walter, Birdbrook, Bocking, Borley, Braintree, Bulmer, Steeple Bumpstead, §Felsted, Finchingfield, Foxearth, Gestingthorpe, Gosfield, Halstead, Castle Hedingham, Sible Hedingham, Great Henny, Lamarsh, Liston, Great and Little Maplestead, †Middleton, Ovington, Panfield, Pebmarsh, Pentlow, Rayne, Ridgewell, Shalford, Stambourne, Stebbing, Stisted, Sturmer and hamlets, Tilbury-juxta-Clare, Twinstead, Wethersfield, Wickham St. Paul, Great and Little Yeldham; *Hinckford Hd.*, clergy and officials.

Essex: *Protestation Returns* continued

Essex Record Office, *Chelmsford* (unless shown as *Colchester* or *Southend*).

See *Essex Family History: A Genealogists' Guide to the Essex Record Office*, Section 14, 'Protestation and Other Returns 1641-44.'

Hinckford Hd.: Microfilm of *H of L* return [T/A 328].

Lists in parish registers (* = transcript at *Society of Genealogists*):
Becontree Hd.: *†Wanstead *(published)*.
Chafford Hd.: *Childerditch *(published)*.
Chelmsford Hd.: †Little Baddow, Boreham *(published)*, †East Hanningfield.
Dengie Hd.: *Dengie *(published)*.
Dunmow Hd.: *†Barnston *(published)*.
Lexden Hd. *[ERO Colchester]:* †Marks Tey, †Wormingford.
Ongar Hd.: †Kelvedon Hatch.
Rochford Hd.: Ashingdon *[ERO Southend]*, *†Hadleigh [microfilm T/R 138/1], Great Stambridge [microfilm 161/1].
Tendring Hd.*[ERO Colchester]:* Great Bentley, †Little Oakley.

Essex continued

Lists in parish registers:
Dengie Hd.: †Dengie.
Dunmow Hd.: †Barnston.
Lexden Hd. *[ERO Colchester]:* †Boxted, †Wormingford.
Ongar Hd.: †Fyfield.
Rochford Hd.: Ashingdon *[ERO Southend]*, †Hadleigh [microfilm T/R 138/1], †Prittlewell [microfilm T/R 182/1].

Lists in parish registers:
Barstable Hd.: Corringham.
Dengie Hd.: Dengie.
Harlow Hd.: †Great Parndon.
Lexden Hd. *[ERO Colchester]:* †Marks Tey.
Rochford Hd.: Ashingdon *[ERO Southend]*, †Hadleigh [microfilm T/R 138/1], †Prittlewell [microfilm T/R 182/1].

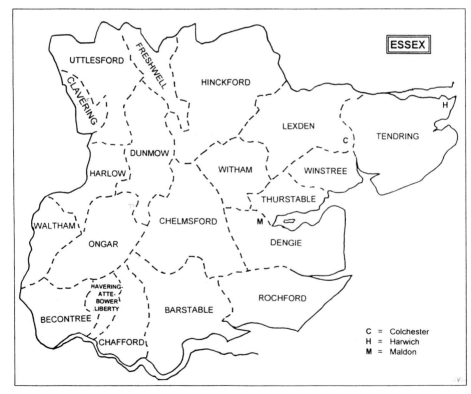

ESSEX

UTTLESFORD
FRESHWELL
CLAVERING
HINCKFORD
LEXDEN
TENDRING
H
C
DUNMOW
WITHAM
WINSTREE
HARLOW
THURSTABLE
WALTHAM
CHELMSFORD
M
ONGAR
DENGIE
HAVERING-ATTE-BOWER LIBERTY
BARSTABLE
ROCHFORD
BECONTREE
CHAFFORD

C = Colchester
H = Harwich
M = Maldon

| Taxation Records |

Public Record Office [E 179].

Subsidy, 1641:
Barstable Hd. (130), some fading. 1 m. [246/3].
Barstable Hd. (400). 4 ms. [112/650].
Barstable (300), **Chafford** (220) **Hds.**; fading. 6 ms. [112/689].
Chafford Hd. (200). 3 ms. [112/667].
Chelmsford Hd. (350), poor in places. 4 ms. [112/657].
Chelmsford Hd. (400). 3 ms. [112/670].
Chelmsford, Dunmow, Freshwell, and Waltham Hds. (est. 700 in all); bad. 6 ms. [112/658].
Colchester (250), fading. 2 ms. [112/660].
Dengie Hd. (125). 3 ms. [112/655].
Dovercourt and **Harwich** (20), poor. 2 ms. [112/651].
Harwich (25). 2 ms. [112/659].
Havering Liberty (100), some fading. 2 ms. [246/4]
Havering Liberty (125). 2 ms. [112/668].
Havering Liberty (120). 2 ms. [112/666].
Hinckford Hd. (500), fading. 5 ms. [112/646].
Maldon Borough (40). 1 m. [112/647].
Maldon Borough and town (50). 1 m. [112/656].
Ongar (100), **Harlow** (50), **Waltham** (50) **Hds.**; very poor. 3 ms. [112/649].
Ongar (350), **Harlow** (200), **Waltham Hds.** (200). 4 ms. [112/663].
Ongar (150), **Harlow** (200), **Waltham Hds.** (50); poor. 4 ms. [112/678].
Rochford Hd. (150). 1 m. [112/645].
Rochford Hd. (200), fading. 3 ms. [112/648].
Rochford Hd. (150). 3 ms. [112/654].
Rochford Hd. (200). 2 ms. [112/677].

Assessment, 1642:
Barstable Hd. (est. 1,250), poor in places. 12 ms. [112/662].
Becontree Hd. (est. 1,000), poor in places. 8 ms. [112/661].
Dunmow (est. 1,000), **Freshwell** (est. 500) **Hds.** 10 ms. [112/653].
Havering Liberty (500). 4 ms. [112/665].
Hinckford Hd. Fragment only. 1 m. [112/679].
Lexden Hd. (est. 1,500). No parishes, names double spaced. 5 ms. [112/652].
Tendring Hd. Very closely written, fading and quite difficult. Two columns for rents and goods. By parish (headings read 'Rate from ...') (2,000). 4 ms. A substantial return, but date uncertain (E 179 calendar has '18 C I' (1642) but 19th century cover has 'Car. II'.

Poll Tax, 1641–42:
Chafford Hd. Too fragile to examine. 8 ms. [246/5]
Havering Liberty. By wards (500). 6 ms. [112/682].

Contributions for Ireland, 1651:
Havering Liberty. Woodford (36). 3 ms. [246/6].

| Collection in Aid of Protestants in Ireland |

There are in fact no surviving parishes in the Collections. 'Berking' turns out to be All Hallows Barking, London, and a list entitled 'Havering Hundred' in the E 179 series turns out to be an account, with no names attached to the actual returns, for two Wiltshire parishes.

GLOUCESTERSHIRE

Parishes: 347.

| Collection in Aid of Protestants in Ireland (9) |

Public Record Office [SP 28/191].

Longtree Hd.: Avening, Cherington, Horsley, Minchinhampton, Rodmarton, Shipton Moyne, Tetbury, Woodchester; one unnamed parish - perhaps Rodborough or Westonbirt, which are also in this Hundred.

| Taxation Records |

Public Record Office [E 179].

Subsidy, 1641:
Gloucester city by wards (200), by parishes (350). 6 ms. [116/519].
Gloucester city by wards (230), by parishes (300). 7 ms. [116/521].
Berkeley Division (400): Thornbury (170), Grumbalds Ash (220), Henbury (160), Langley and Swinehead (20), Pucklechurch (100), Barton Regis (70) **Hds.** 11 ms. [116/525].
Bisley (160), **Whitstone** (250), fading; **Longtree** (150) **Hds.**, fading. 4 ms. [116/524].
Bisley (50), **Whitstone** (300), **Longtree** (200) **Hds.** 4 ms. [116/522].
Bisley (150), **Whitstone** (300), **Longtree** (200) **Hds.**; fading. 5 ms. [116/526].
Cheltenham (700), **Cleeve** (120), **Deerhurst Hds.** (130). 23 ms. in all [116/528 Part 2].
Forest of Dean Division: St. Briavels (150), Botloe (250), **Westbury** (100), **Bledisloe** (100) **Hds.**; some difficult. Probably more Hds. 6 ms. [116/520].
Forest of Dean Division: St. Briavels (130), Botloe (250), **Westbury** (140) and **Bledisloe** (80) **Hds.** 4 ms. [116/523].
Kiftsgate (650), **Tewkesbury** (350), **Tibaldstone** (60), **Westminster** (300) **Hds.**, **Tewkesbury borough** (220) [116/528 Part 1].
Kiftsgate Hd. Lower Division (50), poor. 1 ms. [116/527].

Gloucestershire: *Taxation records* continued

Assessment, 1642:
Berkeley (2,000), some poor; **Grumbalds Ash** (est. 1,000), some poor; **Thornbury** (est. 800) **Hds.** 21 ms. [116/529].

See also 'Names of Gloucestershire gentry in **1657**', J.P. Earwaker, *Gloucestershire Notes & Queries,* **2** (1884), pp. 91-92. List of gentry responsible for collecting the assessment of 1657.

There are no *Protestation Returns* for Gloucestershire at the *House of Lords Record Office.*

HAMPSHIRE (co. Southampton)

Parishes: 307.

Protestation Returns (5)

Returns are extant for Southampton only, none for the remainder of the county.

House of Lords Record Office.

Southampton: Town, corporation and church officials, by ward; wards of Holy Rood, St. Lawrence, St. Michael and St. John, All Saints, St. Mary.

Southampton Archives Service.
Southampton. Indexed transcript, by B. Chincham.

GLOUCESTERSHIRE and BRISTOL

B	= Berkeley (detached)
G	= Gloucester
DofL	= Duchy of Lancaster
LB	= Lower Berkeley
MD	= Middle Dudstone and King's Barton
UL&S	= Upper Langley and Swinehead
UpTew	= Upper Tewkesbury
UpTh	= Upper Thornbury
W	= Westminster

Collection in Aid of Protestants in Ireland (11)

Public Record Office.

Southampton: All SS, Holy Rood, St. Lawrence, St. Michael and St. John [E 179/175/543].
Winchester: St Bartholomew Hide Street, St. Clement, St. Laurence, St. Mary Kallender, St. Maurice, St. Peter Colebrooke Street, St. Thomas [SP 28/192].

Solemn League and Covenant, 1643

Published: 'Some notes on the Solemn League and Covenant in England, with special reference to the parish of **Long Sutton** in Hampshire', C.R. Elvin, *Papers and proceedings of the Hampshire Field Club*, **8**(3) (1919), pp. 271-76. Includes list of those taking this oath in Long Sutton, 1643.

Taxation Records

Public Record Office [E. 179].

Subsidy, 1641:
Alton Division: **Alton** (170), **Selborne** (50), **East Meon** (90), **Finchdean** (150), **Bishop's Sutton** (50) **Hds.** 5 ms. [175/533].
Alton Division: **Alton** (170), **Selborne** (60), **East Meon** (120), **Finchdean** (190), **Bishop's Sutton** (130) **Hds.** 5 ms. [175/542].
Alton Division: **Alton** (200), **Selborne** (60), **East Meon** (130), **Finchdean** (130), **Bishop's Sutton** (100) **Hds.** 4 ms. [175/547].
Andover Division: **Andover** (60), poor; **King's Somborne** (150); **Barton Stacey** (60), poor; **Wherwell** (60) **Hds.**, poor. 3 ms. [175/534].

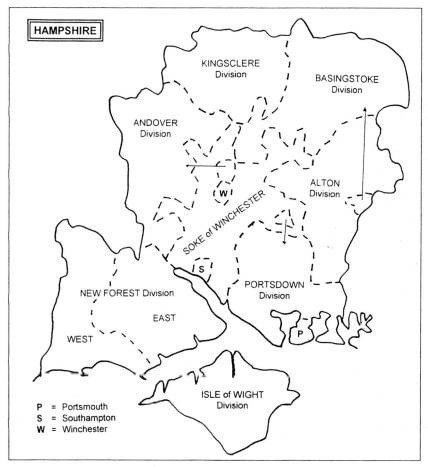

HAMPSHIRE

KINGSCLERE Division

BASINGSTOKE Division

ANDOVER Division

ALTON Division

W

SOKE of WINCHESTER

S

PORTSDOWN Division

NEW FOREST Division

EAST

WEST

P

ISLE of WIGHT Division

P = Portsmouth
S = Southampton
W = Winchester

Hampshire: *Subsidy, 1641* continued

Basingstoke Division: **Basingstoke** (100), **Bermondspit** (50), **Micheldever** (90), **Odiham** (170), **Crondall, Holdshot Hds.** and **Bentley Liberty** (part bad). 3 ms. [175/535].
Kingsclere Division: **Pastrow** (60), **Overton** (40), **Chuteley** (60), **Evingar** (50) **Hds.**; poor in places. 3 ms. [175/548].
Kingsclere Division: **Kingsclere** (60), **Pastrow** (60), **Evingar** (90) **Hds.** 2 ms. [175/550].
New Forest Division: **Christchurch, Ringwood, Fordingbridge, New Forest, Redbridge Hds., Christchurch, Westover, Lymington, Beaulieu, Fawley, Dibden Liberties** (est. 250); difficult and fading. 5 ms. [175/546].
Portsdown Division: **Portsdown** (160), **Bosmere** (50), **Fareham** (80), **Titchfield** (100), **Hambledon** (40), **Bishop's Waltham** (160), **Meonstoke** (70) **Hds., Havant Liberty** (40). 5 ms. [175/536].
Portsdown Division: **Portsdown** (100), **Bosmere** (60), **Fareham** (120), **Titchfield** (50), **Hambledon** 40), **Bishop's Waltham** (130), **Meonstoke** (60) **Hds., Havant Liberty**(40), **Portsmouth Liberty and town** (70). 5 ms. [175/530].
Portsdown Division: **Portsdown, Bosmere, Fareham, Titchfield, Hambledon, Bishop's Waltham Hds., Havant Liberty** (est. 600); very muddled and fading. 4 ms. [175/549].
Isle of Wight Division. Liberties of **East** and **West Medina** (650), bad in parts. 5 ms. [175/537].
Isle of Wight. **West Medina Liberty** (250). 3 ms. First 200 names illegible [175/553].
Soke of Winchester (Fawley Division): **Fawley, Buddlesgate, Mainsbridge, Mainsborough, Bountisborough Hds.** (est. 1,000 in all); fading and all rather muddled. 12 ms. 175/541].
Soke of Winchester: Hds. of **Fawley, Buddlesgate, Mainsbridge, Mainsborough, Bountisborough** (est. 400); all very faded. 8 ms. [175/551].
Southampton town (150). 3 ms. [175/531].
Southampton town (140); one list, bad in parts. 3 ms. [175/538].
Winchester city (190), one list, fading in places. 3 ms. [175/532].
Winchester city (350), one list. 3 ms. [175/544].

Assessment, 1642 (?):
Isle of Wight. Wanting (to conservation in 1989; now no trace). 8ms.+ [175/545].

Poll Tax, 1641:
Kingsclere Division: **Evingar** (250), **Pastrow** (150), **Chuteley** (80), **Overton** (80), **Kingsclere** (150) **Hds.**, of **Whitchurch borough** (50). 6 ms. [247/24].

HEREFORDSHIRE

Taxation Records

Public Record Office [E 179].

Subsidy, 1641:
Broxash Hd. (350), fading in places. 3 ms. [119/459].
Broxash Hd. (300). 2 ms. [237/44].
Ewyas Lacy (150), poor; **Grimsworth** (50); **Webtree** (80) **Hds.**, bad; all difficult. 3 ms. [119/473].
Grimsworth Hd. (150). 3 ms. [119/474].
Ewyas Lacy (70), poor in places; **Webtree** (100) **Hds.**, poor in places. 3 ms. [119/481].
Huntington Hd. (80). 1 m. [119/470].
Huntington Hd. (100). 2 ms. [119/478].
Radlow Hd. (300). 6 ms. [119/469].
Wigmore Hd. (200), a few faded. 2 ms. [237/45].
Wigmore Hd. (200). 2 ms. [119/479].
Wolphy Hd. (300). 2 ms. [119/475].
Wolphy Hd. (300). 6 ms. [119/476].
Wormelow Hd. (250). 3 ms. [119/472],
Wormelow Hd. (250). 4 ms. [119/471].

There are no *Protestation Returns* at the *House of Lords Record Office* and no records of the *Collection in Aid of Distressed Protestants in Ireland* at the *Public Record Office.*

British Library Manuscripts Collection.

Recusants:
1640. Herefordshire recusants indicted [Portland MSS.]. Transcript at **Hereford Record Office.**

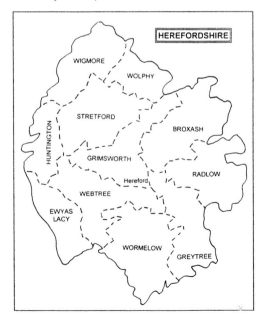

38

HERTFORDSHIRE

Parishes: 132.

Protestation Returns (5)

House of Lords Record Office.

Cashio Hd.: St. Albans (Mayor and other officials;
St. Michael (incl. signatures of those in the house
of the Earl of Sussex) St. Peter, St. Stephen,
Middle Ward, Hollowell Ward);
Redbourn, Sandridge.
No other returns are extant for the county, except
Walkern, below.

Hertfordshire Record Office, Hertford.

Broadwater Hd.: Walkern, in parish register, with
signatures and marks.

Collection in Aid of Protestants in Ireland (85)

Public Record Office
[in SP 28/192 except for Watford, in E 179/121/343].

Broadwater Hd.: Aston, Ayot St. Lawrence, Little
Ayot [St. Peter], Baldock, Benington, Datchworth,
Digswell, Graveley cum Chiffield, [Bishop's]
Hatfield, Knebworth, Letchworth cum Burley,
Great and Little Munden, Sacombe, Stevenage,
Totteridge, Walkern, Watton at Stone, Welwyn,
Weston, Willian, Great and Little Wymondley.

Cashio Hd.: Abbots Langley,
Aldenham, Aldenhamfaldside [?],
Chipping Barnet, East Barnet,
Bramfield [Braintfield], Chorleywood
(Rickmansworth), Codicote, Elstree,
Hexton, Langley [?], Newnham,
Northaw, Norton, Redbourn,
Rickmansworth (three hamlets in
three separate papers), Ridge,
St. Albans: St. Peter, St. Stephen;
Sandridge, Sarratt,
[St. Paul's] Walden, Watford.

Dacorum Hd.: Berkhampstead
[St. Peter], Bovingdon, Bushey,
Caddington, Flaunden, Great and
Little Gaddesden, Harpenden, Hemel
Hempstead, Kensworth, King's
Langley, North Mimms, Northchurch,
Puttenham, Shenley, Shephall,
Studham, Tring, Wheathampstead,
Wigginton; *Dacorum Hd.*

Hertford Hd.: Bayford.

Hitchin and Pirton Hd.: Hitchin,
Ippollitts [St. Ippolyte], Ickleford,
Kimpton, Lilley, Offley, Pirton,
Preston, King's Walden.

Odsey Hd.: Royston (partly in Cambs.).

? Coltsell (hamlet), Willston (hamlet).
No entries for Braughing or Edwinstree
Hds.

Taxation Records

Public Record Office [E 179].

Subsidy, 1641:
Cashio Hd. (550), poor in places. 4 ms. [121/340].
Edwinstree (180), **Odsey** (160) **Hds.** 3 ms.
[121/339].
Edwinstree (200), **Odsey** (160) **Hds.** 3 ms.
[121/342].
Hertford (210), **Braughing** (220) **Hds.** 5 ms.
[121/338].

Assessment (Scottish Loan):
1643/4. Cashio and Dacorum Hds. Two lists by
parish: (1) Voluntary (200); (2) Taxed Lands
(135). There are only a few names in the smaller
parishes. Paper book, 10 folios, rest blank.
[248/19].
1644/5. Cashio and Dacorum Hds. (500). Paper
book. 12 folios. [248/20].
1646/7. County by Hds. with parish against name.
Two lists: (1) dated 16 April 1646;
(2) dated 3 April 1648 (each with 550). Hds. of
Hertford and **Braughing**, Hds. of **Broadwater**
and **Hitchin**, Hds. of **Odsey** and **Edwinstree**
(Cashio and Dacorum seem to be missing).
Smudged and quite difficult. Paper book, 80 folios
(also a 'section money pd outt 1646-50'). [248/21].

HUNTINGDONSHIRE

Parishes: 132.

Protestation Returns (85)

The whole county is covered except for Everton-cum-Tetworth (probably under Biggleswade Hd., Beds., not extant), Hemingford Abbots and Grey, Huntingdon, Offord Cluny, Great Paxton and Yelling. TS index at *Cambs. R.O., Cambridge* and *Huntingdon*, and at *Peterborough Library*.

There are signatures or marks for 30 places, indicated by a dagger (†). Several returns are attached to or on the back of the printed protestation issued to parishes. No returns mention women.

Published: In *Transactions of the Cambridgeshire and Huntingdonshire Archaeological Society*, ed. G. Proby, vol. **5**, pp. 289-368. Ely, 1937; and as *Protestation Returns for Huntingdonshire* (offprint).

Hurstingstone Hd.: †Bluntisham cum Earith, Broughton, Bury, †Colne, †Hartford, Holywell cum Needingworth, Houghton cum Witton, Pidley cum Fenton, Ramsey, Great Raveley cum Upwood, †Little Raveley, Abbots Ripton, Kings Ripton, †St. Ives, Somersham, Great and Little Stukeley, Warboys, Wistow, Woodhurst and Oldhurst.

Leightonstone Hd.: Alconbury cum Weston, †Barham, Brampton, Brington, †Buckworth, Bythorne, Great Catworth, Coppingford cum Upton, Covington, Easton, Ellington, †Great Gidding, Little Gidding, Steeple Gidding, Graffham, †Hamerton, Keystone, †Kimbolton, Leighton, Molesworth, Oldweston, Spaldwick, Stow, Swineshead, Old Weston, Winwick, Woolley.

Norman Cross Hd.: †Alwalton, †Aylton or Elton, †Caldecote, †Chesterton, †Conington, Denton, †Farcet(t), Fletton, †Folkesworth, †Glatton, †Haddon, †Holme, Morborn(e), Orton Long(ueville) [Overton Longville] with Botolphbridge [Bottlebridge], †[Cherry] Orton [Overton Waterville], Sawtrey All Saints, †Sawtrey St. Andrew and St. Judith, †Stanground, Stibbington, Stilton, †Water Newton, †Woodston, Woodwalton, †Yaxley; *Normancross Hd.*, clergy and officials.

Toseland Hd.: †Abbotsley, Buckden, Diddington, Eynesbury, †Fenstanton, Godmanchester, Great Gransden, Hilton, Offord D'Arcey, Little Paxton, St. Neots, Southoe, Great Staughton, †Toseland (parish), Waresley, Hail Weston; *Toseland Hd.*, clergy and officials.

†Swineshead (Leightonstone Hd.) was partly in Bedfordshire, and a Protestation list, presumably in the parish register (at *Bedfordshire Record Office*), was published in *Bedfordshire Parish Registers*, vol. 7 (1933), page 159.

House of Lords Record Office.

Returns as published, above.

Collection in Aid of Protestants in Ireland (10)

Public Record Office [SP 28/192].

Huntingdon: All Saints, St. Benedict, St. John, St. Mary.
Hurstingstone Hd.: Ramsey, Great Raveley, Somersham, Upwood.
Leightonstone Hd.: Kimbolton, Swineshead.

No returns for Norman Cross or Toseland Hds.

Covenant, 1643

Trinity College, Cambridge.

†Swineshead.

Taxation records

Public Record Office [E 179].

Subsidy, 1641:
Leightonstone Hd. (150). 2 ms. [122/217].
Leightonstone Hd. (200), fading. 1 m. [122/221].
Norman Cross Hd. (150). 2 ms. [122/218].
Toseland Hd. (220), poor in places. 3 ms. [122/220].

Assessment, 1642:
Toseland Hd. (est. 1,200). 6 ms. [122/219].

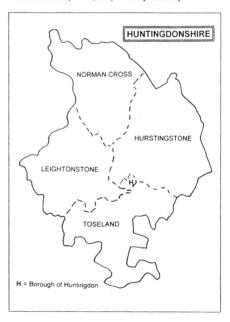

HUNTINGDONSHIRE

NORMAN CROSS

HURSTINGSTONE

LEIGHTONSTONE

TOSELAND

H = Borough of Huntingdon

KENT

Parishes: 400.

Kent: *Collection, Lathe of St. Augustine,* continued

Protestation Returns (91)

House of Lords Record Office.

Returns are extant for most of the north-eastern Lathe of St. Augustine (though little for Canterbury itself) and much of the western Lathe of Sutton at Hone, also for New Romney in Shepway Lathe. The only return with signatures and marks is that for Barfreston, though the Woodnesborough return has some. No returns mention women.

Places for which returns exist are asterisked in the list under the *Collection in Aid of Distressed Protestants,* below. Those for which there are only *Protestation Returns* are shown separately at the end of the hundred concerned.

A microfilm copy of the *Protestation Returns* for Kent is held at *Cumbria Record Office, Barrow-in-Furness* (on the same film as Lancashire returns).

Collection in Aid of Protestants in Ireland (160)

Public Record Office
[in SP 28/192 unless shown otherwise].

Lathe of St. Augustine
Bewsborough Hd.: *Buckland near Dover, Charlton (perhaps Charlton in Sutton at Hone), *West Cliffe, *Coldred, *Ewell, *Guston, Hougham, *West Langdon, *Lydden [E 179/249/10], *River, *St. Margaret at Cliffe, *Sibbertswold, *Whitfield *or* Beaufield [Bewsfield];
Protestation only: *Dover.
Bleangate Hd.: *Chislet, *Herne, *Hoath, *Reculver, *Stourmouth, *Sturry, *Swalecliffe, *Westbere.
Bridge and Petham Hd.: *Bridge (parish); Canterbury - see below; *Lower and *Upper Hardres, *Nackington, *Petham (parish), *Waltham; *Protestation only:* *Patrixbourne.
Canterbury: All Saints, Holy Cross, St. Alphege, St. Andrew, St. George, St. Margaret, St. Mary Bredin (2), St. Mary Bredman, St. Mary Magdalen, St. Mary Northgate, St. Mildred, St. Paul (*Longport), St. Peter; *see also Westgate Hd.;*
Protestation only: *Christchurch (precinct), *Walloon congregation in and about Canterbury.
Cornillo Hd.: East Langdon, Great Mongeham, *Northbourne [Norborne], *Ripple, Sholden, Sutton next Dover.
Downhamford Hd.: *Adisham, *Ickham, *Littlebourne, *Staple, *Stodmarsh, *Wickhambreux [Wickam Brough].
Eastry Hd.: *Barfreston, *Betteshanger, *Chillenden, *Denton, *Eastry (parish), *Eythorn, *Ham, *Knowlton, *Tilmanstone, *Waldershare [a copy of the *Collection* list is in the parish register], *Woodnesborough, *Worth.
Kinghamford Hd.: *Barham, *Bishopsbourne, *Kingston, Wootton.
Preston Hd.: *Elmstone, *Preston juxta Wingham.

Ringslow (or Thanet) Hd.: *Minster in Thanet, Monkton, *St. Lawrence in Thanet, *St. Nicholas at Wade; *Protestation only:* *Birchington, *Margate St. John the Baptist, *St. Peter Broadstairs and Reden Street.
Westgate Hd.: * Canterbury: Holy Cross by Westgate, *St. Dunstan; *Hackington [St. Stephen], *Harbledown [Harbleton], *Thanington [St. Nicholas]; *see also Canterbury.*
Whitstable Hd.: *St. Cosmos and Damian in Blean, *Seasalter, *Whitstable.
Wingham Hd.: *Ash [two returns - one is in E 179/249/11], *Goodnestone, *Nonington, *Wingham (parish), *Womenswold.

Lathe of Aylesford
Maidstone Hd.: Loose.
Shamwell Hd.: Higham.
Toltingtrough Hd.: Gravesend, Milton next Gravesend, Northfleet.

Lathe of Scray
East Barnfield Hd.: Hawkhurst.
Berkeley Hd.: Biddenham.
Blackbourne Hd.: Shadoxhurst.
Calehill Hd.: Charing, Little Chart, Egerton, Pluckley, Westwell.
Chart and Longbridge: Bethersden, Brook, Great Chart, Hothfield.
Cranbrook Hd.: Cranbrook, Frittenden.
Felborough Hd. [all in E 179/249/11]: Challock , Chartham, Chilham, Godmersham, Molash.
Marden Hd.: Goudhurst [E 179/249/9], Marden.
Rolvenden Hd.: Benenden, Rolvenden.
Selbrittenden Hd.: Newenden, Sandhurst.
Wye Hd.: Boughton Aluph, Crundale, Eastwell [a *Protestation* list, with signatures and marks, is in the parish register], Wye.

Lathe of Shepway
Folkestone Hd.: Cheriton, Folkestone, Newington next Hythe; [in E 179/249/10:] Alkham, Capel le Ferne, Hawkinge, Swingfield.
Ham Hd.: Warehorne.
Hayne Hd.: Postling, Saltwood.
Hythe Hd.: Hythe.
Loningborough Hd.: Acrise, Elham, Lyminge.
Newchurch: Ruckinge.
Oxney Hd.: Stone.
Romney Marsh Liberty: Orlestone; *Protestation only:* *New Romney.
Stowting Hd.: Elmsted, Stelling.
Street Hd.: Bonnington, Lympne, Sellinge.

Lathe of Sutton at Hone
Protestation only: *Lower Division, certificate of Justices of Peace.
Axton (Dartford and Wilmington) Hd.: Ash [two returns, one in E 179/249/11], Darenth, Eynsford, Farningham, Longfield, Southfleet, *Sutton at Hone, Swanscombe.

Kent: *Collection,* **Lathe of Sutton at Hone** contd.

Blackheath Hd.: (perhaps Charlton in
St. Augustine), Deptford, (East) Greenwich, Lee,
Lewisham, Mottingham, Sydenham, Woolwich.
Codsheath Hd.: Riverhead;
Protestation only: *Brasted, *Chevening, *Hal-
stead, *Leigh juxta Tonbridge, *Otford, *Deal and
Kensing, *Sevenoaks, *Shoreham, *Sundridge.
Ruxley Hd. [all in E 179/249/11]: Chelsfield, Downe,
Farnborough, Knockholt.
Somerden Hd.: *Cowden [Cowdham]
[in E 179/249/11];
Protestation only: *Chiddingstone, *Groombridge,
*Hever, *Penshurst.
Westerham Hd.: *Protestation only:* *Edenbridge,
*Westerham (parish).

Vow and/or Solemn League and Covenant, 1643

Canterbury Cathedral and City Archives.

In parish records (all with signatures and marks):
Lathe of St. Augustine: Birchington, Ripple,
Stourmouth, Walmer.
Lathe of Scray: Eastwell.

Taxation Records

Public Record Office [E 179].

Subsidy, 1641:
Lathe of St. Augustine
Lathe (150), very bad. 3 ms. [128/620].
Lathe (400), some bad. 8 ms. [128/647].
Lathe (50), poor. 2 ms. [128/656].
Canterbury city by wards (500), fading. 3 ms.
[128/658].
Canterbury city by wards (250), some fading. 3 ms.
[128/654].

Lathe of Aylesford
Lathe (400), badly faded. 3 ms. [128/639].
Hds. of **Shamwell** (150), **Hoo** (30), **Toltingtrough**
(100), **Chatham** (60) **and Gillingham** (40). 6 ms.
[128/642].
Hds. of **Eyhorne** (250), and **Maidstone** (200). 5 ms.
[128/644].
Lathe (est. 500). 2 ms. [128/651].
Hds. of **Shamwell** (120), **Hoo** (40), **Toltingtrough**
(80), **Chatham and Gillingham** (80). 5 ms.
[128/660].
Hds. of **Shamwell** (120), **Hoo** (40), **Toltingtrough**
(100), **Chatham and Gillingham** (80). 5 ms.
[128/661].
Gravesend (150). 4 ms. [272/52].
Rochester and **Chatham** (100). 2 ms. [128/641].
Rochester city by boroughs incl. **Chatham** (120).
3 ms. [128/659].
Lathe of Scray
Hds. of **Cranbrook, [East] Barnfield,
Selbrittenden, Rolvenden, Berkeley,
Blackbourne,** and **Oxney** (400 in all, double
banked and difficult). 5 ms. [128/638].
Hds. of **Milton** (200), **Teynham** (50), **Faversham**
(110), **Boughton** [under Blean] (40), fading, mixed
and difficult. 6 ms. [128/640].
Hds. of **Milton, Teynham, Faversham, Boughton**
[under Blean] (500 in all), three columns of closely
written names; some fading. 2 ms. [128/648].
Lathe of Shepway
Hds. of **Folkestone** (Upper and Lower) (100) and
Loningborough (Upper and Lower) (100) and
part of *Lathe of Scray* (est. 600). 4 ms. [128/643].
Lathe of Sutton at Hone
Upper division
(600), some poor.
6 ms. [128/645].
Upper division
(500). 6 ms.,
some paper.
[128/646].
Hds. of **Codsheath**
(100),
Somerden (70),
Westerham (70)
with **Brasted**. 2
ms. [128/649].
Upper division
(est. 600), poor in
parts. 6 ms.
[128/650].
Lower division
(300). 3 ms.
[128/657].

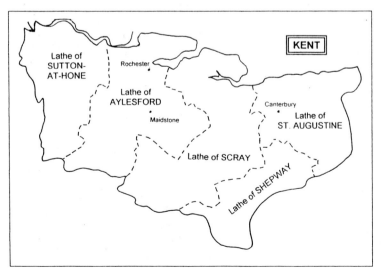

Kent: *Taxation records* continued

Poll Tax Assessment, 1641:
Parish of **Wilmington** (75), 'all about 16 years or 26 years of age'; town of **Lewisham** (200). Gives name of householder plus wife/father/daughter/ lodger if applicable. 2 ms. [249/12].

Assessments etc. 1642-46:
1642. Eythorne and **Maidstone Hds.** (Lathe of Aylesford). Two columns, lands and goods by parish (600) (fragment). This gots progressively poorer the further into the ms. 4 ms. [128/662].
1642. Rochester. Assessment (loan) (80). 3f. [128/663].
1643. Aylesford (lathe, northern division). Assessment (subsidy). By hd. and parish (incl. city of Rochester) (2,500-3,000). The first two ms. are poor; fading in parts. 31 ms. [128/653].
1643. Milton (this is presumably Milton near Gravesend, not Milton near Sittingbourne nor Milton near Canterbury). Assessment (Earl of Essex's army). Two columns, lands and goods (300). 4 ff. [128/667].
1643. Woolwich. List of estates (50 names, as to lands and goods). Much altered, ?draft. 2 ff. [128/668].
1643. North Cray. Assessment (fragment) (9 names only, rest missing) [249/15].
1644. East Greenwich. Particulars of account (levy for defence). Lists holders of land on left with names of tenants and occupiers of land opposite (850+). 15 ms. [237/63].
1645. St. Mary Cray. Assessment. Names of land holders and tenants. Rent, tax, estates. 40 holders of land, three times as many when including tenants. 2 ms. [249/18].
1646. Eythorne and **Maidstone Hds.** Account of contributions (from Caleb Bankes) (250). 8 ms. [249/19]

LANCASHIRE

Parishes: not calculated, due to townships.

Protestation Returns

Returns are extant for all hundreds except the northern Lonsdale Hundred.

Women are more frequently mentioned than in any other county: 11 places in Amounderness Hd.; 15 in Blackburn Hd.; 3 in Leyland Hd. and one each in Salford and West Darby Hds. Places which include women are marked §. Often there are only a few, widows in particular. There are family groups at Brearcliffe (widows only), Burnley, Croston and Eccleston.

Occupations, marked ‡, are given at Goosnargh, Altham, Clayton, Brindhill, Chorley, Croston, Euxton, Shevington, Rivington and Anglezarke. The return for Croston (and its townships) is outstanding, including women, relationships and occupations. No returns have signatures and marks.

***Published:* Salford Hd.:** Flixton: *A History of Flixton, Urmston and Davyhulme,*
by D.H. Langton, n.d.;
Manchester: *Palatine Note Book,* vol. **1,** p. 80 et seq., Manchester, 1881; *Manchester Genealogist,* 1971; *Manchester Genealogist,* **30,** 1994.
Newton: *The History of Newton Chapel,*
by H.T. Crofton (Chetham Society Publications, vol. **52,** New Series vol. **1**), 1904;
Rochdale: *The History of the Parish of Rochdale,*
by Henry Fishwick, pp. 541-54, Rochdale and London, 1889;
Salford: *Palatine Note Book,* vol. **4,** pp. 100-111, Manchester, 1884; *Manchester Genealogist,* 1971-74.
West Derby Hd.: *Atherton,* by John Lunn, n.d.;
Liverpool: *Inhabitants of Liverpool from the 14th to the 18th Century,* by R. Stewart-Brown, 1930.

House of Lords Record Office.

Amounderness Hd.: Aston cum Hothersall; Bispham with Layton and [Black]pool; Bleasdale, Fulwood, and Myerscough; Broughton; Garstang, with Barnacre, Bilborough, Catteral, Claughton, Wyersdale; ‡Goosnargh, Newsham, and Whittingham; §Kirkham, with Bryning cum Kellamurgh, §Clifton cum Salwick, §Freckleton, Greenalgh cum Thistleton, §Larbrick cum Eccleston, Medler cum Wesham, Newton cum Scales, §Ribby cum Wrea, Singleton Magna cum Parva, Treals cum Roseacre, §Warton, §(2) Westby cum Plumptons, §Weeton, Wharles; Lytham; §Pilling; Poulton le Fylde with Carlton, Hardborn cum Newton and Marton; Preston; §St Michael on Wyre; Stalmine; §Wood Plumpton.
Blackburn Hd.: Blackburn (parish and places therein: Balderstone, Billington, Clayton le Dale, Lower and Over Darwen, Little Harwood, Livesey, Mellor cum Eccleshill, Osbaldeston, Pleasington, Risheton, Salesbury [Salisbuerie],

Lancashire: *Protestation Returns, Blackburn Hd.*
Blackburn ctd.:Tockholes [Tockoles], Walton in the
Dale and Overdale, Wilpshire [Lipshire] cum
Dinkley, Yate with Pickup Bank [Pictoppbanke];
list of certain inhabitants of some of the above-
named places who refuse to take the protestation:
Chipping; Ribchester, including Alston, Dilworth,
Dutton);
Whalley (parish and places therein: Accrington,
§(22) ‡Altham, §(4 widows) Aighton Bailey, Bacup
[Bacobb], §(widows) Briercliffe [Brearcliffe],
§Burnley, Chaigley [Chadgley], Chatburn§
(widows), Church Kirk with Osbaldwistle, ‡Clayton
supra Moras§ (some), Clitheroe (borough),
§(8) Cliviger, §(some), Colne (incl.Trawden Forest,
Fowlridge, Marden Magna), §Downham,
Dunnockshaw [Dunkinhalgh], Extwistle,
§(3) Goldshaw [Goodshawe], §Habergham Eaves,
§(5) Hapton, Haslingden, Heyhouses, Ightonhill
Park, Mearley, Mitton with Henthorne and
Clocotes, Newchurch in Rossendale, §Newchurch
in Pendle, §(5 widows) Padiham, Pendle,
Pendleton, Reade, §Reedley Hallows (incl. Filley
Close, Newland), §(3 widows) Simonstone,
Wiswell, Worsthorn cum Hurstwood, Worston).
Leyland Hd.: ‡Brindle [Brindhill];
‡Chorley;
‡§Croston, with ‡§Bretherton, ‡§Byspham,
‡§Hesketh cum Becconsall [Beconsfaild],
‡§Mawdesley, §Rufford, ‡§Tarleton, ‡§Walton;
§Eccleston, with Heskin, Parbold, Wrightington;
§Hoole;
Leyland (parish), with Clayton, Cuerden, ‡Euxton,
Hoghton (with Withnell, Whealton and Heapey),
Whittle-in-le-Wood;
Penwortham, with Farrington, Hutton [Houghton],
Howick, Longton;
Standish, with Adlington, Anderton, Coppull,
Charnock Heath, Charnock Richard, Duxbury,
Langtree, ‡Shevington, Welch Whittle,
Worthington.
Salford Hd.: Ashton under Lyne (incl. townships);
Bolton, including Great and Little Bolton,
Breightmet [Brightnett], Haulgh [Haigh], Harwood,
Little Lever, Darcy Lever, Lostock, Sharples,
Tonge, Edgeworth, Entwistle, Quarlton,
Longworth, Turton, Blackrode, ‡Rivington with
‡Anglezarke [Anlesarghe];
Deane, including Farmworth, Haliwell, Heaton,
Horwich, Little, Middle and Over Hulton, Kersley,
Rumworth [Romworth], Westhaughton;
Bolton and Deane parishes, clergy and officials;
Bury, including Cowpe, Edenfield [Eatenfield],
Lench, Musbury, Newallhey, Shuttleworth;
Bury and Ratcliffe (parishes), clergy and officials;
Lower Tottington;
Radcliffe;
Middleton, including Ainsworth, Birtle (with Bamford
and Ashworth), Hopwood, Great Leaver,
Pilsworth, Thornham;
Rochdale, including Butterworth, Castleton,
Huddersfield, Spotland *(published?)*;

Lancashire: *Protestation Returns, Salford Hd.* ctd.
Manchester *(published?)*, including Ardwick, Birch,
Blackley [Blakeley], Cheetham, Chorlton
[Chollerton] cum Hardy (with Haghend,
Mansleache, and Hardie), §(2 widows) Chorlton
Row, Crumpshall [Crumsall], Denton, Didsbury
(with Withington, Burnage, and Levenshulme),
Eccles, Flixton *(published)*, Gorton, Harpurhey
[Harpar Hay], Haughton, Heaton Norris, §Newton
Heath (with Droylsdon, Bradford, and Failsworth)
(published?), Openshaw;
Manchester (parish), clergy and officials;
Prestwick cum Oldham, including Alkrington
[Akerington], Heaton-upon-Faughfield, Oldham,
Tonge, Outwood within Pilkington, Unsworth
within Pilkington, Whitfield within Pilkington;
Reddish;
Stretford;
Salford and liberties *(published?)*.
West Derby Hd.: Leigh, with Astley, Atherton
(published), Bedford, Pennington, Tyldesley cum
Shackerley, Westleigh;
Liverpool;
Wigan;
Winwick, including Arbury, Ashton, Croft,
§(7) Culcheth, Goulborne, Houghton, Hulme,
Lowton cum Kenion, Middleton, Newton,
Southworth.

Lancashire Record Office, Preston.
[Microfilm MF 1/25; Photocopy P 147].

Amounderness Hd.: microfilm and photocopy.
Blackburn Hd.: microfilm.
Leyland Hd.: microfilm; Croston (photocopy).
Salford Hd.: microfilm.
West Derby Hd.: microfilm.

Cumbria Record Office, Barrow-in-Furness.

Microfilms as at *Lancashire Record Office.*

Manchester Central Library (Local Studies).

Salford Hd.: Oldham and Middleton parishes:
transcript [MF 651] (probably mf of next entry).

Oldham and Manchester History Library.
Salford Hd.: Middleton: Giles Shaw Mss. Vol. 18,
pp. 37-73.

Collection in Aid of Protestants in Ireland

There are no returns for Lancashire in the
Collection in Aid of Distressed Protestants in Ireland.
However, it is suggested that the return filed
under Norfolk [SP 28/195] as Norwich St. Helen
should in fact be for St. Helens in Lancashire.

Lancashire continued

Taxation Records

Public Record Office [E 179].

Subsidy, 1641:
Amounderness Hd. (including poll tax on recusants) (est. 1,500). 31 ms. [131/333].
Amounderness Hd. (including poll tax on recusants) (est. 1,500). 29 ms. [132/336].
Amounderness Hd. (recusants excused poll tax on ground of poverty) (400). 6 ms. [132/338].
Amounderness Hd. (150); fragile in parts; only a few names per parish. 3 ms. [132/346].
Leyland Hd. (800). 13 ms. [131/335.
Leyland Hd. (certifcate of defaulters) (250), one list with comments as to default. 4 ms. [250/3].
Leyland Hd. (50), fragment only. [132/341].
Lonsdale Hd. (including poll tax on recusants) (500). 10 ms. [132/337].
Lonsdale Hd. (80), fragile. 2 ms. [132/342].
Salford Hd. (300), quite poor. 6 ms. [132/339].
Salford Hd. (500). 7 ms. [131/334].
West Derby Hd. (includes names of recusants) (800). 8 ms. [132/340].

Assessment, 1642:
Amounderness Hd., fragment only. 1 m. [132/344].
Leyland Hd. (including poll tax on recusants); paper, too fragile to examine. 4 ms. [132/340a].
Lonsdale Hd., Furness and Cartmel Liberty (130) (Assessment loan). 3 ms. [132/343].
Lonsdale Hd., fragment only. 1 m. [132/345].
West Derby Hd. (1,250). 16 ms. [131/332].

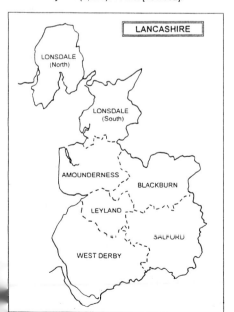

LEICESTERSHIRE

Parishes: 256.

Protestation Returns (5)

Published: East Goscote Hd.: Gaddesby;
Guthlaxton Hd.: Bitteswell, Frolesworth;
Sparkenhoe Hd.: Aylestone.
All in Phillimore's *Leicestershire Marriage Registers*, vol. 5, pp. 145-151.

Leicestershire Record Office, Wigston Magna.

Returns in original parish registers, as published; also:
Sparkenhoe Hd.: Appleby (Magna).

There are no returns for Leicestershire at the House of Lords Record Office.

Collection in Aid of Protestants in Ireland (66)

Public Record Office
[SP 28/192 except where shown otherwise].

Framland Hd.: Branston [SP 28 194/4 with Staffs.], Stathern, Stonesby [Stockney?].
Gartree Hd.: Blaston, Husbands Bosworth, Burrough [on the Hill], Gumley, (Market) Harborough, Kibworth Beauchamp and Harcourt, Houghton (on the Hill) [E 179/266/21], Owston and Newbold, Pickwell, Saddington, Scraptoft, Smeeton Westerby, Theddingworth.
East Goscote Hd.: Barrow on Soar [E 179/251/15], Caldwell and Trickham [?] [E 179/251/29], Cossington, Frisby on Wreak [E 179/251/29], Ragdale [E 179/251/29], Ratcliffe on the Wreak, Reasby [E 179/251/29], Satchfield, Saxelby [E 179/251/29], Seagrave, Warnaby [E 179/251/29], Wymeswold [Wimeswould] [E 179/134/309].
West Goscote Hd.: Woodhouse (Barrow upon Soar) [E 179/134/310].
Guthlaxton Hd.: Arnesby, Bitteswell, Broughton Astley, Great and Upper Claybrooke, Cosby, Dunton Bassett, Foston, Frowlesworth, Little Peatling.
Leicester: All Saints, St. Margaret, St. Martin, St. Mary, St. Nicholas.
Sparkenhoe Hd.: Barlestone, Barwell, Sparkenhoe, Cadeby, Dadlington, Higham in Linley [?Higham on the Hill], Ibstock, Kirkby Mallory [SP 28/194 under Staffs.], Markfield [SP 28/194/4 under Staffs.], Nailstone in Barton, Newbold Verdon, Odeson, Peckleton [SP 28/194/4 under Staffs.], Ratcliff Culey, Stoke Golding, Sutton Cheney, Thornton, Ullesthorpe [Ullestrayne ?].

? Dalby Chalcombe;
Caldwell and Trickham [E 179/251/29] - see under East Goscote Hd.,
Stockney - see Stonesby in Framland Hd.;
Ullestrayne - see Ullesthorpe in Sparkenhoe Hd.;
also three unidentifed places.

Leicestershire continued

Taxation Records

Public Record Office [E 179].

Subsidy, 1641:
Sparkenhoe, West Goscote, Guthlaxton Hds.
(est. 500), very difficult in places. 9 ms. [134/306].

Assessment, 1642:
Leicester borough by wards (800). 5 ms. [134/305].
Framland Hd. (300), fading and with holes. 3 ms.
[134/307].

LINCOLNSHIRE

Parishes: 627

Protestation Returns (374)

Returns for rather over half the county are extant.
In **Holland** all three wapentakes or hundreds are
represented. In **Kesteven**, Boothby Graffoe,
Langoe, Flaxwell, Aswardham and Grantham Soke
are wanting, and there is only one return for
Loveden. In **Lindsey**, Bolingbroke, Candleshoe,
Gartree and Wraggoe are wanting.

Over fifty places in **Lindsey** (none in Holland or
Kesteven) have signatures and marks, indicated by
a dagger (†).

Occupations are given in Roxby and Hemswell.

Women are listed at Hemswell (in family groups)
and Muckton. Grayingham, Waddington St. Peter
and Glentworth Spittle Session each have two
women (presumably widows and/or householders).

Lincolnshire: *Protestation Returns* contd

Places duplicated in the *Collection in Aid of
Distressed Protestants in Ireland* are asterisked, but
these, with the exception of two attached to
Protestation Returns, have not been published.

Published: *Protestation Returns 1641/2 - Lincoln-
shire*, transcribed and published by W.F. Webster,
Mapperley, Nottingham, 1984.
Places giving clergy and officials only are in *italics*.

Parts of Holland
Elloe Wapentake: Cowbit, Crowland [Croyland],
Gedney, Gedney Fen, Holbeach, Lutton in Sutton,
Moulton, Spalding, Sutton St. Edmund, Sutton St.
James, Sutton St. Mary, Tydd St. Mary, Weston,
Whaplode, Whaplode Drove.
Kirton Wapentake: Algar Kirk [Algarkirk], Bicker,
Brothertoft, Donington, Fosdyke, Frampton,
Gosberton [Gosberkirk], Kirton, Quadring,
Sutterton, Swineshead, Wigtoft, Wyberton.
Skirbeck Wapentake: Boston, Butterwick, Fishtoft,
Freiston [Frieston], Leake, Wrangle.

Parts of Kesteven
Aveland Wapentake: Aslackby (incl. Graby,
Milnethorpe and Avethorpe), Billingborough
[Billingborow], Bourne Dyke and Cawthorpe,
*Dembleby cum Willoughby, Dowsby, Dunsby,
*Folkingham [Falkingham], Haceby, Hacconby
cum Stainfield [Steinfield], Horbling (incl.
Bridgend), Kirkby Underwood, Morton, Newton,
Osbournby, *Pickworth, *Pointon cum Membris,*
Rippingale, *Semp(e)ringham, Spanby, Swaton,
*Threckingham (incl. Stow), *Walcot (near
Folkingham); clergy and officials - see *Winnibriggs
and Threo Wapentake.*
Beltisloe Wapentake: Basingthorpe cum Westby,
Bitchfield, Burton Coggles, Castle Bytham cum
Counthorpe (see also Swinstead), Little Bytham,
Careby, Corby, *Creeton* (see also Swinstead),
Edenham cum Membris, Gunby, Holywell and
Aunby (members of Castle Bytham), Irnham with
Bulby and Hawthorpe, Lenton or Lavington
[Levington] (incl. Osgodby, Hanby, and Keisby
[Keasby]), *Lound*, Skillington, Stainby, Swayfield
(near Bitchfield), Swinstead (incl. Castle Bytham
and Creeton), North Witham [esqs., gents.,
husbandmen, cottagers, sons and servants],
*Witham on the Hill cum Membris; clergy and
officials - see *Winnibriggs and Threo Wapentake.*
Lincoln Liberty: *Bracebridge, *Branston,
*Canwick, **Lincoln** city (clergy and officials), *St.
Benedict, *St. Botolph, *St. Margaret's within the
Close, *St. Mark's, *St. Martin's, St. Mary
Magdalen (within the Close), *St. Mary Magdalen
within the Bayle, *St. Mary Wigford, *St. Michael
on the Hill, *St. Nicholas in Newport, *St. Paul's,
*St. Peter at the Arches, *St. Peter in Eastgate,
*St. Peter in the Gowts, *St. Swithin; *Waddington.
Loveden Wapentake: Hougham.

46

Ness Wapentake: Barholm(e) [shows servants], Baston, Brace-borough, Carlby [Carelbie], Market Deeping, Deeping St. James, West Deeping, *Greatford (Gretford) (Col. attached and pub'd.), Langtoft, Stowe, *Tallington*, Thurlby, Uffington, *Wilsthorpe (Col. attached and pub'd.); clergy and officials, see *Winnibriggs and Threo Wapentake.*

Winnibriggs and Threo Wapentake: East and West Allington, *Barrowby, *Boothby Pagnall*, *Heydour* [Hayther], Honington, (Great) Humby [Humby Magna], *(Little) Ponton [Paunton Parva]*, *Ropsley, Sedgebrook, Somerby (near Grantham), *Spittlegate, (North) Stoke, Stroxton, *Syston, Welby, *Wilsford, *Woolsthorpe [Woolstrop]; *Winnibriggs and Threo, Beltisloe, Ness and Aveland Wapentakes*, clergy and officials.

Parts of Lindsey

Aslacoe Wapentake: Bishop's Norton, Blyborough [Blyburgh], Caenby [Cannbye], †Cammeringham [Camringham], Coates, Cold Hanworth, †Filling-ham, Glentham in Spittle Sessions, Glentworth (Spittle Session), †Hackthorn, Hemswell [family groups, incl. women, and occupations], †Ingham, †Normanby (by Spittal), Owmby, †Saxby, Snitterby, †Spridlington, Willoughton.

Bradley Haverstoe Wapentake: Ashby-cum-Fenby, Aylesby, Barnoldby le Beck, Beelsby, Bradley, Brigsley, †Cabourne, Cleethorpes, Great and Little Coates, North Coates, Cuxwold, Fulstow Marsh, Grainsby, Hatcliffe, Hawerby with Beesby, Healing, Holton, Humberstone, Ir(e)by, Laceby, Wold Newton, †East Ravendale [Randall], †Rothwell, Scartho, Swallow, Swinhope, Tetney, North Thoresby (two returns), Waithe, Waltham.

Lawres(s) Wapentake: Aisthorpe [Aistropp cum Thorpe], Barlings, Brattleby, Broxholme, Burton-next-Lincoln, North and South Carlton, Cherry Willingham, Dunholme-juxta-Welton, Falding-worth, †Fiskerton, Friesthorpe [Frysthorpe], Gre(e)twell, Nettleham [Netham], †Reepham, Saxilby [Saxelbie], Scampton, Scothern(e), Snarford, †Sudbrooke and Holme, Torksey cum Hardwick, Welton juxta Lincoln.

Calceworth Hd.: †Aby, Alford (incl. Rigsby and Ailby), Anderby, †Calceby, †Claxby, †Gayton in the Marsh, Hogsthorpe, †Mablethorpe, †Maltby in the Marsh, Mumby Chapel, Strubby cum Woodthorpe, Theddlethorpe St. Helen, Thrusthorpe or Trusthorpe [Trustropp].

Corringham Wapentake: †Blyton, Cleatham (cert. only), Corringham (parish), †**Gainsborough**, †Grayingham, Heapham, Kirton-in-Lindsey, Laughton by Gainsborough, †Lea, Morton (in Gainsbrough), Northorpe [Northrope], Pilham and Gilby, Scotter, Scotton-cum-Ferry, Springthorpe with Sturgate, *(East) Stockwith, Walkerith*; *Corringham Wapentake*, clergy and officials.

Hill Hd.: Ashby Puerorum, Aswardby, †Bag Enderby, Brinkhill, Claxby Pluckacre, Fulletby, Greetham, Hagworthingham, †Hameringham, Harrington, Langton, South Ormsby cum Ketsby, †Oxcombe, Salmonby [householders and others], Sausthorpe, Scrafield, *†Somersby, Tetford, Winceby.

Louth Eske Hd.: Alvingham, Authorpe, †Burwell cum Walmsgate, †Calcethorpe cum membris [Calstropp] (two returns), Castle Carlton, †Great and Little Carlton, †Cockerington St. Mary or North Cockerington, †Conisholme, North and South Elkington, †Farforth with Maidenwell, Gayton-le-Wold, Grainthorpe [Garnthorp] with Wragholme, †Grimoldby, Hallington, Haugham, Keddington, Kelstern, †**Louth**, Manby, †Muckton [women named], Raithby cum Maltby, North Reston, †Ruckland, Saltfleetby (All Saints, †St. Clement, St. Peter), †Skidbrook, North Somerco(a)tes, †South Somerco(a)tes, Stewton, Tathwell, Welton (le Wold) juxta Louth, Withcall [shows cottagers and servants], Yarburgh [Yarborough]; *Louth Sessions*, clergy and officials.

Ludborough Wapentake: Covenham (†St. Bartholomew, St. Mary), †Fotherby (incl. Little Grimsby and Brackenborough), Ludborough, North Ormsby, †Utterby, Wyham cum Cadeby.

Manley Wapentake: Alkborough or Auckborough [Auckborrow] cum Walcot, Althorpe (with Burringham), Appleby, Belton [incl. French inhabitants], Bottesford (with Ashby, Butterwick, Burringham, and Yaddlethorpe), Broughton, †Burton upon Stather, West Butterwick (in Owsten), Crowle (with Ealand, Eastoft and Tetley), Epworth, Flixborough, Frodingham (with Brombey and Crosby), West Halton (with Coleby), Haxey (incl. Eastlound, Craiselound, Westwoodside and Burnham), Hibaldstow, Luddington cum Garthorpe, Manton (with Cleatham and Twigmore), Messingham, Owston (Melwood Park or High Melwood), Redbourne, †Risby cum Sawcliffe, Roxby [occupations given], Scawby cum Sturton, Waddingham (St. Mary, St. Peter), Whitton, Winteringham, Winterton, Wroot.

Walshcroft Wapentake: Binbrook (St. Gabriel, St. Mary, Claxby by Normanby (on the Hill), Croxby, South Kelsey (St. Mary, St. Nicholas), Kingerby, Kirkby-cum-Osgodby [Osgood], Linwood [householders, sons, servants], Newton by Toft, Normanby le Wold (Normanby on the Hill), †Market Rasen [East Rasen], Middle Rasen, †West Rasen, Stainton-le-Vale (le-Hole), Tealby (Tevelby) Thoresway, Thorganby, Thornton-le Moor, Toft (next Newton), Usselby, Walesby, †North Willingham.

Well Wapentake: Brampton, Gate Burton, Kettlethorpe with Laughterton and Fenton, Knaith, Marton, Newton on Trent, Stow (St. Mary's), Upton cum Kexby (cert. only), Willingham juxta Stow; *Well Wapentake*, clergy and officials.

Yarborough Wapentake: Barnetby (le Wold), Barrow (on Humber), Barton on Humber (St. Mary, St. Peter), Bigby (with Kettleby, Thorp, Glamford Briggs or Glanford Bridge), Bonby, Brocklesby cum Little Limber, Cadney cum Howsham [Housham], Caistor, Clixby, †Croxton, †Elsham, South Ferriby, Goxhill, Grasby [Gresby], Habrough [Haburgh], East Halton, Holton le Moor, Horkstow, Immingham, Keelby [Keilbye], North Kelsey, Killingholme, Kirmington, Great Limber [Limburgh Magna], Melton Ross, Nettleton, Riby, †Saxby (All Saints), Searby [Serby] with Owmby, Somerby juxta Bigby, Stallingborough, Thornton Curtis [esqs., gents., yeomen, husbandmen], Ulceby [Ulseeby], †Wootton, Worlaby [Worletby], Wrawby (also Bigby, Glamford Briggs adjacent to Wrawby).

House of Lords Record Office.

Returns as published, above.

Collection in Aid of Protestants in Ireland
(38)

Places duplicated in the Protestation Returns are asterisked.

Published (in *Protestation Returns*):
Kesteven, Ness Wapentake: *Greatford (Gretford), *Wilsthorpe [these two places are on the same pieces of paper as the Protestation Returns at the *House of Lords Record Office*].

Public Record Office [SP 28/192].

Parts of Kesteven
Aveland Wapentake: *Dembleby, *Folkingham, *Pickworth, *Semp(e)ringham, *Threckingham, *Walcot (near Folkingham).
Beltisloe Wapentake: *Witham on the Hill.
Lincoln Liberty: All places as shown above under Protestation Returns except for Lincoln St. Mary Magdalen within the Close.
Winnibriggs and Threo Wapentake: *Barrowby. Belton juxta Grantham, Boothby (Pagnell), **Grantham**, *Heydour cum membris, Little Ponton, *Ropsley, Spittlegate, *Syston, *Wilsford, *Woolsthorpe.

Parts of Lindsey
Hill Hd.: *Somersby.

Unidentified: Cillingborough; Hornington [? Horsington, Gartree (Lindsey) Wapentake, in SP 28/195, listed as Warwickshire in error].

Lincolnshire continued

Taxation Records

Public Record Office [E 179].

Subsidy, 1641:
Town of **Boston** (100). 3 ms. [140/735].
Wapentakes of **Manley** and **Corringnam** (100) poor. 1 m. [140/736a]. Dated **1643** [?].

Assessment, 1642:
Parishes of **Wispington** (20), **Cawkwell** (50), **Tattershall** (50), town of **Tumby** (60). 8 ms. [140/734[.
Wapentake of **Boothby-Graffoe** (500). 9 ms. [140/732].
Wapentake of **Loveden** (450). 5 ms. [140/733].
Wapentake of **Skirbeck** (900). 6 ms. [140/736].
Wapentakes of **Corringham** (1,200), **Well** (400) and **Lawres** (1,300). Mixed as to areas. 17 ms. [140/729].
Lincoln by wards (650). 4 ms. [140/731].
Parish of **Goltho** with hamlet of Bullington (15). 1 m. [140/747].
Soke of **Horncastle**, wanting (last seen 1990). 2 ms. [140/743].
Parish of **Helton Holgate** (30). 1 m. [140/765].

Lincolnshire: *Taxation records* continued

House of Lords Record Office [Main Papers, 22 Dec. 1641].

Poll Tax certificates, 1641:

Parts of Kesteven

Lincoln city: north, east, south and west wards, the close, the bailey.

Aswardhurn Wapentake: Asgarby cum Boughton, Aswarby, Aunsby, Burton Penwardine, Culverthorpe, Evedon, Ewerby cum Austrop, Great and Little Hale, Heckington, Helpgringham, Howell, Ingoldsby, Kelby, Kirkby-le-Thorpe, South Kyme, Quarington, Scredington, Swarby, Silk Willoughby.

Flaxwell Wapentake: Anwick, Ashby, Bloxholm, Brauncewell cum Dunsby and Temple Bruer, Cranwell, Digby, Dorrington, Holdingham, Leasingham, North Rau(n)ceby, Rowston, South Rau(n)ceby cum Handbeck, Ruskington, Sleaford.

Langoe Wapentake: Billinghay, Blankney, Dockdike, Dunston, Potter Hanworth, Heighington, Kirkby Green, North Kyne, Martin (*recte* in Well Wapentake), Metheringham, Nocton, Thorpe Tinley, Timberland, Scopwick, Walcot(t), Washingborough.

Parts of Kesteven

Bradley Haverstoe Wapentake: parishes as under Protestation Returns *plus* Grimsby Magna, Holton [Howton in] le Clay, Marsh Chapel.

Corringham Wapentake: (names but no parishes differentiated).

Manley Wapentake: (parishes as under Protestation Returns *plus* Conesby [Coningsby in Soke of Horncastle?], *less* Cleatham, Melwood, Sturton, Walcot, Wroot, and Yaddlethorpe).

Walshcroft Wapentake (names but no parishes differentiated).

Well Wapentake (names but no parishes differentiated).

Yarborough Wapentake (Caistor Sessions): (parishes as under Protestation Returns less Bigby and Halton le Moor [East Halton?].

There are also certificates, but no lists of names, for *Parts of Lindsey:* Aslacoe Wapentake, Caistor Sessions, Lawres and Louth Wapentakes; *Parts of Kesteven:* Boothby Graffoe Hundred and Loveden Hundred; and *Parts of Holland:* Boston Borough.

CITY OF LONDON

Parishes: 102.

Protestation Returns (7)

Guildhall Library (parishes marked with a dagger (†) have signatures and marks; women (§) are included in St. Mary Magdalen Milk Street and St. Stephen Coleman Street (Vow and Covenant)).

Churchwardens' accounts: †Holy Trinity the Less [Ms 4835].

Vestry minutes: †St. Katherine Cree (5 May 1641) [Ms 1196/1, pp. 30-34]; †St. Martin Orgar [Ms 959/1]; †§St. Mary Magdalen Milk Street [Ms 2597]; St. Matthew Friday Street (3 June 1641) [Ms 3579, pp. 339-41]; St. Pancras Soper Lane (5 May 1641) [Ms 5019/1].

There are no *Protestation Returns* for the City of London at the *House of Lords Record Office*.

Vow and Covenant, 1643 (‡)
Solemn League and Covenant, 1643/4 (*)

Guildhall Library (see above for † and §).

Churchwardens' accounts:
(‡ or *) †St. Benet Fink [Ms 1303/1];
‡*†St. Clement Eastcheap [Ms 977/1].

Vestry minutes: *St. Bartholomew by the Exchange [Ms 4384/2, p. 12]; *St. Olave Jewry [Ms 4415]; ‡*St. Stephen Coleman Street (‡‡(some) § June 1643; * Dec. 1643?) [Ms 4458/1].

Collection in Aid of Protestants in Ireland (71)

Public Record Office [SP 28/193 unless shown otherwise].

All Hallows Barking (two lists, one filed under Essex in error); All Hallows Bread Street; All Hallows the Great; All Hallows Honey Lane; All Hallows Lombard Street; All Hallows London Wall; All Hallows (.....); Bridewell; Christ Church; East Smithfield liberty in St. Botolph Aldgate; Holy Trinity; St. Andrew Holborn; St. Andrew Undershaft; St. Andrew by the Wardrobe; St. Anne and St. Agnes; St. Antholin; St. Augustine; St. Bartholomew by the Royal Exchange; St. Bartholomew the Great; St. Bartholomew the Less; St. Benet Fink; St. Benet Paul's Wharf; St. Botolph Aldersgate [E 179/252/14]; St. Botolph Aldgate; St. Botolph Billingsgate; St. Botolph Bishopsgate; St. Bride; St. Clement Eastcheap; St. Dunstan in the East; St. Dunstan in the West; St. Edmund the King; St. Ethelburga; St. Gabriel Fenchurch; St. Gregory; St. James Duke's Place; St. James Garlickhythe; St. John the Baptist; St. John the Evangelist; St. Katherine by the Tower; St. Katherine Coleman; St. Katherine Creechurch; St. Lawrence Poultney; St. Leonard Foster Lane; St. Magnus; St. Margaret (.....); St. Margaret Lothbury; St. Margaret Moses; St. Margaret New Fish Street; St. Margaret Pattens; St. Martin Ludgate;

City of London: *Collection* continued

St. Martin Outwich; St. Mary Bothaw; St. Mary Somerset; St. Mary Staining; St. Mary Woolchurch; St. Matthew Friday Street; St. Michael le Querne; St. Michael Paternoster Royal; St. Michael Queenhithe; St. Michael Wood Street; St. Mildred Bread Street; St. Mildred Poultry [part in E 179/252/14]; St. Nicholas Acons; St. Nicholas Cole Abbey; St. Pancras Soper Lane; St. Paul (two lists); St. Peter Westcheap; St. Sepulchre; St. Swithin; St. Vedast; Whitefriars.

Taxation Records

Publications: *The Inhabitants of London in **1638**, ... from MS.272 in the Lambeth Palace Library*, ed. T.C. Dale, Society of Genealogists, M'fiche 1995 (also 'A directory of London in 1638', *Genealogists' Mag.* **1**, 1925, pp. 7-8; discussion of a document which lists tithepayers in 93 city parishes).
*List of the Principal Inhabitants of the City of London, **1640**, ed.* W.J. Harvey. Blackmansbury offprints **1**. Pinhorns, 1969. Originally published Mitchell & Hughes, 1886, and also in *Misc. Gen. et Her.*, 2nd series **2**, 1888, 35-7, 51-3, 68-72, 85-8, 107-10, 114-6 [?from P.R.O. E 179/251/22].

Public Record Office [E 179]

*?Subsidy, **1641**:*
Farringdon Within Ward (memorandum of defaulters). 1 m. [251/20].
Broad Street Ward (memorandum of defaulters) (20), paper. 3 ff. [251/21].
St. Austine, St. Nicholas Cole Abbey, St. Peter (Paul's Wharf) and **St. Mary Magdalene (Old Fish Street)** (schedule of inhabitants and freemen) (300). 8 ff. [276/55].

*Assessment Poll Tax, **1641**:*
London City Companies. Twenty seven City Companies are listed with approximately 7,000 names, mostly with their members' location or parish of residence. The numbers vary from 10 in the case of Woolmen to 1,200 Leathersellers. Some show defaulters but the lists seem far from up-to-date and notes indicate this in that *"many may bee dead."*
 The Companies listed include Barbers and Surgeons, Blacksmiths, Bowyers, Black Bakers, Butchers, Coopers, Cordwayners, Drapers, Farriers, Fishmongers, Fletchers, Fruiterers, Girdlers, Glaziers, Haberdashers, Horners, Leathersellers, Lorimers, Mercers, Paviors, Pewterers, Scriveners, Skinners, Turners, Vintners, White Bakers and Woolmen. 293 ms. [251/22]. *?Published.*
Aldersgate Ward (1,000 names including family and servants, with occupations) and parish(?) of St. Martin's le Grand (170 family units with another 80 with occupations described *as those men that are free in the said liberty*). Paper. 87 ff. [252/1; transcript at Society of Genealogists].

City of London: *Assessment, Poll Tax, **1641*** ctd.

Bassishaw Ward (200 family units), paper and fragile.10 ff. [252/2; transcript at Society of Genealogists, MX G/108].
Billingsgate and **Lime Street Wards**, mostly conserved fragments. Then better run, mostly in Billingsgate (600). 90 ms. [252/3; transcript at Society of Genealogists, MX G/106].
Parishes of **St. Benet Fink** (10), **St. Christopher** (50), **Allhallows and St. Martin Outwich** (100). 8 ms. [252/4].
Parishes of **St. Stephen Coleman Street** (list of 52 family units incl. servants), very fragile; and **St. Olave Old Jewry** (24 family units with names of servants and lodgers). 17 ms. [252/5+; transcript at Society of Genealogists, MX G/108].
Parish of **St. Mary Colechurch** (50), surnames only. Mr... with occupations. 2 ms. [252/6].
Parishes of **St. Mary Aldermary** and **St. Olave Silver Street** (60), paper and poor. 11 ff. [252/7].
Dowgate Ward (500 family units), rather scrappy. 33 ms. [252/8; transcript at Soc. of Gen [MX G/105].
Parish of **St. Matthew Friday Street**. Freemen (30 names) 1 m. [252/9; transcript SofG, MX G/106].
Farringdon Ward. Parish of **St. Sepulchre** (800/1,000 family units naming occupants by their abode: courts, alleys etc.). Also Old Bayley (sic) (400 names). 68 ff. paper [252/10; transcript at Society of Genealogists, MX G/107].
Lime Street Ward (200 family units and 130 Freemen). 22 ff. paper. [252/11; transcript at Society of Genealogists, MX G/106].
Langbourne Ward (600 names and lists of Freemen), some gaps. 18 fs. paper. [252/12; transcript at Society of Genealogists, MX G/106].
Walbrook Ward. Parishes of **St. Mary Woolchurch Haw** (30 family units), **St. Stephen (Walbrook)** (40 family units), **St. Mary Bothaw** (20 family units). 6 ms. [252/13; trans at SofG MX G/108].

Assessment (subsidy):
1641. Bassishaw Ward (50), partially illegible. 2 ms. [147/566].
1641. Cornhill Ward (120). 3 ms. [147/568].
1641. Cheap Ward (250), poor. 5 ms. [147/572].
1642/3. Certs of non payment. 16ms. [147/574]:
 (1) St. Giles Without Cripplegate; some street names (250);
 (2) All Hallows Barking; tiny writing (220);
 (3) St. Botolph without Bishopsgate (part of Broad Street Ward) (40);
 (4) London Bridge (?) (50);
 (5) St. Dionis Backchurch (35);
 (6) St. Martin's Ludgate and Christchurch (125);
 (7) St. Peter Westcheap, St. Matthew Friday Street, St. Leonard's Foster Lane, St. Augustine, St. Michael Le Querne and St. Faith under St. Paul's (40);
 (8) St. Martin Pomary (Ironmongers Lane), St. Mary Colechurch and St. Pancras (50);
 (9) St. Dunstan in the East and Tower Ward (50);

City of London: *Assessment (non payment)* contd.

(10) St. Mary Le Bow and St. Lawrence Jewry (30);
(11) St. Mary Woolnoth, St. Nicholas Acon, St. Edmund the King and St. Clement (75);
(12) St. Anne Blackfriars; tiny writing (100);
(13) St. Alphage, St. Alban and St. Mary Magdalen, Milk Street (30);
(14) St. Peter Le Poer and All Hallows, London Wall (25).
Various portions of assessment much fragmented and partially not examined. [147/578]

Parliamentary Assessment, 1642:
London by Wards. Names of assessors and persons assessed for the raising of moneys for the defence of the Kingdom, King and Parliament. A book of 88 pp., faded; comments as assessment and to abatement, exemption or payment. 2,000/2,500 names. [147/577].
Often detailed description of goods. Remarks such as *"Goods sould of his for £20.12s." "The collectors say there was a chest with plate etc. carried to Guildhall."*
Aldersgate, Al(d)gate, Bishopsgate, Bridge, Broad Street, Billingsgate, Bread Streete, Bassishaw. Cornehill, Cripplegate Within, Cripplegate Without, Castle Baynard, Candlewicke, Colman Streete, Cheape, Cornwayner, Dowgate, Farringdon Without, Farringdon Within, Langborne, Limestreete, Portsoken, Queenshithe, Tower, Vintrey, Walbrooke, Saviours, Olaves, Georges, Thomas.

Parliamentary Assessment, 1645/6:
Farringdon Without; nearly illegible. 3 ms. [147/576].
Candlewick Street Ward (110); incls. Clements Castleheane[?], Leonards Precinct, Michaells East and West. 2 ms. [147/579].
Tower Ward (250); incls. Dolphin Precinct, Mincing Lane, Salutation Precinct, Rood Precinct, Dice Key Precinct, Beare Key Precinct. 5 ms. [147/580].
Walbrook Ward (150) incls. Salters Hall (fading), Swithens Precinct, Mary Woolchurch, Batchelors in the Stockes? 3 ms. [147/581].
Cordwainer Street Ward (est. 100); very poor. 3 ms. [147/582].
Billingsgate Ward (160); incls. Mary at Hill; some poor Buttolphes. 3 ms. [147/583].
Cordwainer Street Ward (100); incls. Pancras Bennetts and John, Thomas and Trinity Precinct. 2 ms. [147/584].
Cheapside Ward (200), some poor and badly faded; incls. Mary le Bowe, Laurence Lane, Catt Eaton. 3 ms. [147/585].
Farringdon Without Ward (120), incls. Whitneyfeilds,?? Chauncery Lane?; rest illegible. 3 ms. [147/586].
Vintry Ward (150); poor in places; incls. Thomas Noves?? (Apostles?) and Trinity, Michaell Royall and John's Precinct. 3 ms. [147/587].

City of London: *Parl. Assessment 1645/6* ctd.

Dowgate Ward (180); some lost; incls. Little All hallowes Precinct, Laurence Pountney. 3 ms. [147/589; transcript at Soc. of Gen., MX G/105].
Many mutilated scraps but incls. **Queenhithe Ward** (70), gaps and poor; Peter's and Queens Precincts. 3 ms.
Tower Ward (250); incls. Dolphin Precinct, Ironmonger Lane, Allmemgr? Lane Precinct, Salutation Precinct, Dice Key, Ralphs Key, Beare Key. 3 ms. [147/590].
Billingsgate Ward (120), poor. Andrewes. 3 ms. [147/591].
Walbrook Ward (125), quite poor; incls. Stephens Precinct, John's Precinct, Marie Abchurch. 3 ms. [147/594].
Al(d)gate Ward (450); incls. Creechurch Parish, Leadenhall Street, Raven Alley, The Streete, Sugar Loaf Alley, Brownes Alley, Axe Alley, Church Lane, Poor Jury Lane, Bliss's Court, George Alley, Katherine Coleman, Fenchurch Street Northside, Ralphs Rents, Northumberland Alley, Back Alley, Pye Alley, Allhallows Steyning Blanchappleton Court. 6 ms. [147/595].
Farringdon Without Ward (300). Alleys and Courts (poor). 4 ms. [147/596].
Bishopsgate Ward (100), some faded; Peters Cornhill, Martins Outwich Precinct. Allhallows Precinct. 3 ms. [147/597].
Portsoken Ward (150); incls. Hounditch Precinct, Covent Garden (Gravel Lane). 3 ms. [147/598].
Farringdon Without Ward: St. Bridge alias Brides Precinct (70), poor. 3 ms. [147/599].
Farringdon Without Ward. St. Martin Ludgate (80) poor 2 ms. [147/600].
Walbrook Ward. Swithin's Precinct (130); incls. Mary Woolchurch, The Batchelors in the Stocks. 3 ms. [147/601].
Aldgate Ward (350); incls. St. Andrew's Undershaft (part), poor. Courts and Alleys, St Olave. Hartstreet, St James Duke Place (part), London Wall, Liberty of Heneage and Bevis Marks. 5 ms. [147/616].
Account Book *for the contribution of the value of one meal in the week.* Paper book, 96 ms. (Ordinance of Parliament, 28th March 1644). 24 Wards as in 147/577 (2,650 names). The amounts vary from 4s. to £20 indicating rank of individual (or inflated for status purposes). A further 170 names without residence. *Payment being discharged* [252/15].

Guildhall Library, Department of Manuscripts.

Subsidies, Aids etc., 1630-65:
St. Bartholomew by the Exchange [MS 4384/2].

Lambeth Palace Library

Tithes, 1638:
Tithepayers in 93 city parishes [MS.272]. *Published.*

MIDDLESEX

Parishes: 67.

Protestation Returns (60)

Returns are extant for much of the county (but not the City of London).

Published: The following parishes (ed. A.J.C. Guimraens) are in Supplements to the *British Archivist,* vol. **1**, London, 1913-20, pp. 1-88 and *Miscellanea Genealogica et Heraldica,* 1921; republished on microfiche by North Middlesex FHS, 1987.

Ossulstone Hd.: Clerkenwell (St. James), Finchley, Friern Barnet, Hampstead, Hornsey (and Highgate), Islington (and Stoke Newington), St. Giles Cripplegate, St. Sepulchre, Shoreditch (St. Leonard), Willesden; **Tower Division:** Bromley (St. Leonard), Stepney, Limehouse (with street names), Poplar and Blackwall, Ratcliff, Stratford Bow, Old Ford, Spitalfield, Bethnal Green, Mile End;

Edmonton Hd.: Edmonton (parish), Enfield, (Monken) Hadley and South Mimms.

Other publications:

Elthorne Hd.: West Drayton and Harmondsworth: 'The protestation returns for West Drayton and Harmondsworth', S.A.J. McVeigh, *West Drayton and District Historian,* **31** (1969), pp. 5-9.

Spelthorne Hd.: Hampton: *People and Homes in Hampton-on-Thames in the 16th and 17th centuries,* B. Garside, Hampton, the author, 1956. Sunbury: '"As far as I lawfully may": the protestation returns of 1641', Richard Chapman, *West Middlesex FHS,* **12**, 1 (March 1994).

House of Lords Record Office.

Returns for New Brentford, Greenford Magna, Hayes, and Bromley St. Leonard's (part) have signatures and marks (†). The return for Stratford-le-Bow includes women.

Places duplicated in the *Collection in Aid of Distressed Protestants in Ireland* are asterisked.

Edmonton Hd.: *Edmonton, *Enfield, (Monken) Hadley, *South Mimms, *Tottenham. *Mostly published, see above.*

Elthorne Hd.: †(New) *Brentford, Cowley, *Cranford, *West Drayton *(published),* †Greenford Magna, Greenford Parva), *Hanwell, Har(e)field, *Harlington, Harmondsworth *(published),* †Hayes [Heese], Hillingdon, Ickenham, Northolt [Northall], *Norwood, *Ruislip, Uxbridge [Woxbridge]; *Elthorne Hd.,* clergy and officials.

Gore Hd.: *Edgware, *Harrow, *Hendon, Kingsbury, Pinner, *(Great) Stanmore [Magna], *(Little) Stanmore [Parva] [Whitchurch alias]; *Gore and part of Ossulstone Hd.,* clergy and officials.

Isleworth Hd.: Heston, Hounslow, *Isleworth, *Twickenham.

Ossulstone Hd.: Clerkenwell (St. James), Finchley, *Friern [Fryern] Barnet, *Hampstead, *Hornsey and Highgate, Islington and Stoke Newington, St. Giles Cripplegate, St. Sepulchre, Shoreditch (St. Leonard), Willesden; for clergy and officials see under *Gore Hd. Published, see above.*

Ossulstone Hd., Tower Division: †Bromley St. Leonard's, Limehouse, Stepney and hamlets (*Ratcliff, *Whitechapel), Stratford-le-Bow; *Ossulstone Hd., Tower Divison,* clergy and officials. *Published, see above.*

Spelthorne Hd.: Ashford, *(East) Bedfont, *Feltham, *Hampton on Thames *(published),* *Hanworth, Laleham, Littleton, Shepperton, Staines, Stanwell, *Sunbury *(published),* *Teddington.

Collection in Aid of Protestants in Ireland (37)

Public Record Office [SP 28/193 unless shown otherwise].

Places duplicated in the *Protestation Returns* are asterisked.

Edmonton Hd.: *Edmonton, *Enfield, *South Mimms [E 179/253/8], *Tottenham.

Elthorne Hd.: *(West) Brentford, *Cranford, *West Drayton, *Hanwell, *Harlington, *Norwood, *Ruislip.

Gore Hd.: *Edgware, *Harrow (2), *Hendon (2), (Great and Little) Stanmore.

Isleworth Hd.: *Isleworth, *Twickenham.

Ossulstone Hd.: *Friern Barnet, Chelsea, Ealing, *Hampstead, *Hornsey, *Ratcliff (in Stepney), St. Giles in the Fields [filed under 'London'], Stepney *see Ratcliff,* Stoke Newington, Whitechapel (upper hamlet).

Spelthorne Hd.: * (East) Bedfont, *Feltham, *Hampton and Hampton Wick, *Hanworth, *Sunbury, *Teddington.

Westminster: St. Margaret [filed under 'London'].

Taxation Records

See *Guide to Middlesex Lay Subsidies, 1500-1645,* C. Webb. Research aids series **21**, West Surrey FHS, 1990. This lists records at the P.R.O.

Published: Harrow on the Hill, 'The inhabitants of Harrowe and its neighbourhood in 1642', George Grazebrook, *Middlesex and Hertfordshire Notes & Queries,* **3** (1897), pp. 136-39.

Public Record Office [E 179].

*Subsidy, **1641**:*
Edmonton (270), **Gore** (160) **Hds.** 4 ms. [143/312].
Elthorne Hd. (60), goods and lands. 2 ms. [143/319].
Elthorne Hd. (50). 2 ms. [143/319].
Isleworth Hd. (200), poor. 1 m. [143/310].
Ossulstone Hd. (100), poor. 1 m. [143/314].
Ossulstone Hd. (100), poor. 1 m. [143/316].
Spelthorne Hd. (200), poor. 2 ms. [143/311].

Middlesex: *Taxation records* continued

Assessment, 1642:
Ossulstone Hd. (calendar says 'County' but only Hundred) [143/323].
 This Consists of 49 double sided Ms. bound in one Roll with an estimated 8,000/10,000 names with detailed locations of assessments as to Goods and for Lands. It is generally in good condition apart from the first two Ms. The places mentioned are not inclusive. The original spelling is retained but can usually be identified in a modern context.
Parishes of St. Sepulchres (poor), St James (poor), Islington, Clarkenwell Close, St. John's Jerusalem, Turnemill Street (poor), Naked Boy Alley, Jacobs Court, Barber's Alley, Bowling Alley, Black Lyon Alley, Three Horshoes Alley, White Horse Alley, Legetall? Yard, Redd Lyon Alley, Cinnamon Alley, Black Spread Egle Alley, Mutton Lane, Parsons Alley, Bull Head Alley, Ragg Lane, Edward's Rents, Surplassage Passage, St. Gyles Cripplegate, Grub Street (some mutilation), White Cross Street, Red ? Cross Street, Golding Lane, Old Street, Canon Burie, Prebend Hould, Newington Burrough, St. John Jerusalem in Tower, Barnesburie, Barnesbury Wharf, Upper and Lower Holloway, Tollingoon, Outdwellers, Fryan Barnett, Hornsey, Stoke Newington, Trinitie Minoris, Ratcliffe, Shadwell, Wappinge Wall, Ratcliffe Highway, Lower Wapping, Ratecliffe, Popler and Blackwall, Lymhowse, Milles his Rents, East Smithfeild, Whitechappell, Wentworth Street, High Street North Side, Streetside, Petticoate Lane, Brick Lane, Southeswell, Church Lane, Goodman's Yard and Feilds, Peacock Alley, Rosemarie Lane, Alyens, Hoxton Streete, Hollowell Street, Moorfeilds, Church End, Haggerston, Hoxton, Spittlefeilds, Hackney, Mare Street Newington, Shacklewell, Clapton, Hamerton, Darleston, Well Street, Grove Streete, Mile End, Bow and Old Ford, St. Leonard's Bromley, Land Golders, Tower Liberty within the Tower, In the Mynt Yeoman Warders, Tower Hill, Tower Liberty without the walls, Without the Posborne (Postern), Tower Wharf, The Bulwark, Without Bulwark, Tower Dock, Platts Bride, Hall Bride, St. Katherine's, Tower Baulke, Wapping in the Walls(?), Wapping Land Side, Shadwell, Sharpes Alley, Norton.
Ossulstone Hd. (Friern Barnet) (70). 1 m. [143/313].
Ossulstone Hd. (defaulters) (est. 1,000), street names. Paper, difficult. 20 ms. [253/11]. **'1643'**.
Ossulstone Hd. (defaulters) sometimes with the reason for such default [poor, gone away etc.]; incl. Chancery Lane and Rolls Liberty (35), St. Giles in the Fields (150), streets mentioned, and a few in Hammersmith, Chiswick, Kensington, hamlet of Saffron Hill, Marylebone, Hampstead, Holborn, Ealing (names lost), Acton, Kentish Town. 17 ff. [143/317]. Dated **1643/4.**
Finchley (150), paper; poor. 1 m. [143/323a].
Friern Barnet (100). 1 m. [143/325].
Parish of **Hackney** (500), very faded. 3 ms. [253/7].

Middlesex: *Assessment* continued

Yeoman Ward of the **Tower** (certificate of defaulters) (40). 1 m. [143/315].
Ward of the **Tower**, etc. (est. 150), too fragile to examine. 3 ms. [143/324].
Westminster (defaulters): St. Margaret's (140), St. Martin-in-the-Fields (250), Savoy (12), St. Clement Danes (15). 15 ms. [143/338].
Westminster (defaulters): St. Margaret's (50), St. Martin-in-the-Fields (200), by streets. [143/318].

Army Assessment:
1645. Islington. Liberties of Cannonbury (50) and Barnsbury (60), Prebend (30), Newington Canon (20), Newington Green (20), Holloway (40), Out Dwellers (40). 16 ms. [253/13].
1643-46. Parish of **St. Giles in the Fields.** Several years (300 and 400). 12 ms. [253/14].

Other Taxes:
1641-47. Westminster: 21 ms. [253/10]:
(1) Poll tax accounts (1641) with occupations, locations, names of servants (400; figures show 80% of assessment was abated).
(2) Disbanding army (1641) (125).
(3) Providing fortifications (1646) (125) and defaulters (1646) (75).

City of Westminster Archives Centre,
10 St Ann's Street, London SW1P 2XR.

Assessments:
1644 (Army Rate). St. Margaret's Westminster.
1645 (Army). St. Margaret's [E 1580].
1646 (Scottish Army). St. Martin-in-the-Fields [F 3347].
1647 (Relief of Ireland). St. Margaret's [E 1624].
1647 (Army in Ireland). St. Margaret's [E 1581].
1647-53 (Army Rate). St. Margaret's.

MONMOUTHSHIRE
No relevant records appear to survive.

NORFOLK

Parishes: 691.

Protestation Returns

Published: East Rudham, in 'Protestation oath at East Rudham, 1641/2', H.J. Dukinfield Astley, *Norfolk Parish Register: Marriages, 8, Phillimore's Parish Registers Series, 202* (1914), pp. 151-53.

Norfolk Record Office, *Norwich.*
Note. The Record Office is temporarily closed consequent on the fire at Norwich Central Library on 1st August 1994.

According to David Cressy, in *Literacy and the Social Order*, 1980, parish records for the following four parishes included lists with signatures and marks (†), either for Protestation or Covenant; and possibly one other parish (without signatures and marks). It has not been possible to check these:

†Breccles, †Eaton [parish covenant, Case 13/62], †Hassingham [parish register PD 88/1], Little Plumstead, [PD 123/49], †South Walsham [parish register, PD 252/1].
East Rudham, in parish register, as above.

There are no Norfolk returns at the *House of Lords Record Office.*

Collection in Aid of Protestants in Ireland (245)

Public Record Office [all in SP 28/194; in four boxes, parts 3 and 4 as indicated].

Blofield Hd.: Blofield, Bradeston, Brundall, Buckenham cum Hassingham, Burlingham (St. Andrew, St. Edmund, St. Peter), Cantley, Limpenhoe, Lingwood, and Little Plumstead, North Postwick, Southwood, Strumpshaw, Thorpe near Norwich.

Clavering Hd.: Brooke, Bergh [Burgh] Apton, Ellingham next Bungay, Howe, Kirby Cane, Norton sub Course, Raveningham, Thurlton.

Depwade Hd.: Aslacton, Bunwell, Forncett St. Mary.

Diss Hd.: Frenze, Gissing, Scole [Osmondiston], Shimpling, Thelvedon, Tivetshall St. Margaret.

North Erpingham Hd.: Gunton.

Eynesford Hd.: Bintree cum Twyford.

West Flegg Hd.: Billockby, Hemsby, Martham, Repps cum Bastwicke, Rollesby, Thurne [Thirne], Winterton cum East Somerton.

Gallow Hd. *[asterisked places in Part 3]:* Bagthorpe, Barmer [Bermer], East Barsham, North Barsham, West Barsham, *Broomsthorpe [Brunsthorp and Tattersett] with Daughton, Fulmodestone, Helhoughton, *Hempton, (New) Houghton near Harply, Houghton near Harply, West Houghton, Kettlestone, (Pudding) Norton, East Rainham, South Rainham, (West) Rainham [St. Margaret], East and West Rudham, Great and Little Ryburgh, Sculthorpe, Shereford, Little Snoring, Stibbard, Syderstone, Tatterford, Toftrees.

Norfolk: *Collection* continued

South Greenhoe Hd. *[asterisked places in Part 3]:* *South Acre, *Bodney, East and West Bradenham, *Cockley Cley, *Great and Little Cressingham, *Didlington, *Foulden, *Gooderstone, *Hilborough, *Holme Hale, Houghton next North Pickenham, Narborough [Narburgh], Narford, Newton by Castle Acre, *Oxborough, *North and *South Pickenham, *Shingham, Sporle, *Swaffham.

Happing Hd. *[all except Palling in part 3]:* Brumstead, Catfield, Happisburgh, Potter Heigham, Hempstead, Hickling, Ingham, Lessingham, Palling, East Ruston, Stalham, Walcott; two unidentified parishes (perhaps Horsey and Sutton).

Launditch Hd. *[all in Part 3]:* Beeston, Beetley, East Bilney, Little Bittering, Brisley, Colkirk, East Dereham, Great and Little Dunham, North Elmham, Great and Little Fransham, Gateley, Gressenhall, Hoe, Horningtoft, Kempston(e), East and West Lexham, Litcham, Longham, Mileham, Oxwich, Rougham, Scarning, Stanfield, Swanton Morley, Tittleshall cum Godwick, Weasenham All Saints and St. Peter, Wellingham, Wendling, Whissonsett, Worthing.

King's Lynn Borough: King's Lynn *[in Part 3].*

Mitford Hd. *[all in Part 3]:* Hardingham, Hockering, Letton, Reymerston, Shipdham, East and North Tuddenham, Westfield, Woodrising, Yaxham.

Norwich Borough: Earlham, Heigham, Lakenham; **Norwich:** Cathedral, Dutch congregation, St. Andrew *[SP 28/194 pt 3 but filed in LDR A.490]*, St. Benedict, St. Etheldred, St. George Tombland, St. Giles, St. Gregory, St. Helen *[SP 28/195, but ? in error for St. Helen's, Lancs.]*, St. James within the Gates, St. John Maddermarket, St. John of Sepulchre, St. John Timberhill, St. Julian, St. Lawrence, St. Margaret, St. Martin at Oake, St. Michael at Pleas, St. Michael at Thorne, St. Michael of Coslany, St. Peter Hungate, St. Peter Permountegate, St. Peter Southgate, St. Simon and St. Jude, St. Stephen, St. Swithin; one unidentified Norwich parish; Eaton, Trowse Milgate.

Smithdon Hd. *[asterisked places in Part 3]:* *Great Bircham, *Bircham Newton, *Bircham Tofts, *Brancaster, *Docking, *Fring, *Heasham, *Holme (next the Sea), *Hunstanton, Ingoldsthorpe, *Ringstead, Sedgeford, Shernborne, Snettisham *[SP 28/194 pt. 3 but filed in LDR A.490]*, *Stanhoe, *Thornham, *Titchwell.

Taverham Hd. *[all except Hellesdon in Part 3]:* Attlebridge, Beeston St. Andrew, Catton, Crostwick, Drayton, Felthorpe, Hellesdon, Hors(e)ford, Horstead with Stanninghall, Rackheath, Salhouse, Sprowston, Wroxham.

Thetford Borough: Thetford.

Tunstead Hd. *[* = Part 3; ** = Part 4]:* *Ashmanhaugh, *Barton Turf, *Beeston St. Lawrence, **Bradfield, **Crostwight, *Edingthorpe,

Norfolk: *Collection,* continued

Tunstead Hd. contd. ******Felmingham, *****Honing, ******Horning, ******Instead, ******Neatishead, *****Ridlington, ******(Sco') [South] Ruston, *****Sloley, *****Smallburgh, *****Tunstead, *****North Walsham, ******Westwick, *****Witton, ******Worstead.
Walsham Hd. *[all in Part 4]:* Acle, Beighton, Haltergate, Moulton (St. Mary), Reedham, Tunstall.
Yarmouth Borough: Great Yarmouth.

Solemn League and Covenant, 1643-44

House of Lords Record Office.

1643/4 (March) **-1644** (April). **South Erpingham Hd.:** Aylsham [Aylisham], Baconsthorpe, Little Barningham, Blickling, Buxton, Cawston, Colby, Cottishall, Erpingham, Great Hautbois, Heydon, Lammas, Oxnead, Saxthorpe, Skeyton, Stratton Strawless [Stralis], Thwaite, Tuttington.
Lists of inhabitants 'who have taken the Covenant'. (from *H.M.C. Appendix to 6th Report*, pp. 8-10).

Norfolk Record Office, Norwich (see note p. 54).

†Eaton parish covenant [Case 13/62].

Taxation Records

Public Record Office [E 179].

Subsidy, 1641:
Diss (150), fading in parts; **Earsham** (200); **Henstead** (150); **Depwade** (200) **Hds.** 6 ms. [153/617].

Norfolk: *Subsidy, 1641* continued

South Erpingham and **Eynesford Hds.** (est. 1,500); crumbling. 15 ms. [253/37].
South Greenhoe (200), **Wayland** (100), **Grimshoe** (100), **Guiltcross** (100), **Shropham** (130) **Hds.**; some fading. 8 ms. [153/619].
Borough of **Thetford** (40). 1 m. [153/620].
Borough of **Thetford** (40). 1 m. [153/621].

For the Relief of the Army, 1641:
Hds. of Depwade (100), lands and Henstead (100), lands. [154/669a].

Assessment, 1642:
Henstead Hd. (800), some faded. 4 ms. [153/624].
Borough of **Thetford** (170). 2 ms. [153/622].
Borough of **Thetford** (190). 3 ms. [153/623].
Borough of **Yarmouth** (with certificate of defaulters) by wards (400). 3 ms. [153/625].
Borough of **Yarmouth** (350), some faded. 2 ms. [153/628].

Norfolk Record Office, Norwich (see note p. 54).

Subsidy assessments:
1641, March. Hundreds of **Wayland, Grimshoe, Shropham, Guiltcross, South Greenhoe** [WLS XVII/2, 410 x 5].
1643. **Gallow Hd.:** South Raynham (parish); **Launditch Hd.:** Beetley, Horningtoft, Scarning (parishes) [MC 431/5, 734 x 7].

See also 'Norwich subscriptions for the regaining of Newcastle, 1643', F.R. Beechino, *Norfolk Archaeology,* **18** (1914), pp. 149-60.

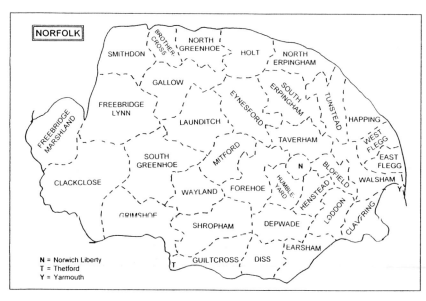

NORTHAMPTONSHIRE

Parishes: 292

Protestation Returns

Published: Guilsborough Hd.: Long Buckby
(probable Protestation list), as part of earliest
parish register, *Vaughan Papers in Adult
Education No. 17*, University of Leicester, 1971,
pp vii, 74-76.

Northamptonshire Record Office, Northampton.

Lists in parish registers:
Guilsborough Hd.: Long Buckby. *Published.*
Hamfordshoe Hd.: Great Doddington [105p/1].
Higham Ferrers Hd.: Irchester [177p/E/Ir/B1].
Nobottle Grove Hd.: East Haddon [Misc. photostat
749].
Rothwell Hd.: Marston Trussell [B(MT)313].
King's Sutton Hd.: Brackley St. Peter (possible
Protestation list).

No returns at *House of Lords Record Office.*

Collection in Aid of Protestants in Ireland (5)

Published: King's Sutton Hd.: Aynho, Croughton,
in 'Aynho and Croughton Inhabitants in 1642', by
J.S.W. Gibson, *Cake & Cockhorse* (Banbury Hist.
Society), vol. **10**, no. 1 (Autumn 1985), pp. 17-18.

Public Record Office [SP 28/194 pt. 1].

King's Sutton Hd.: Aynho (published), Brackley St.
James, Brackley St. Peter, Croughton (published),
Whitfield.

Taxation Records

Public Record Office [E 179].

Subsidy, 1641:
Town of **Northampton** (130); one list. 2 ms.
[157/421].
Hds. of **Corby** (150), **Rothwell** (100), **Higham
Ferrers** (100), some fading; **Hamfordshire** (70);
Huxloe (180), some bad; **Polebrook** (100);
Orlingbury (100); **Navisford** (40). 10 ms.
[157/423].
Hds. of (**King's**) **Sutton** (100), some poor;
Wymersley (120); **Green's Norton** (50); **Nobottle
Grove** (80); **Fawsley** (120), some fading;
Spelhoe (60); **Cleley** (80); **Chipping Warden**
(40); **Guilsborough** (150). 13 ms. [157/422].
Various, Chas I, not examined [157/433-438], **n.d.**

Assessment(?), 1642:
Town of **Northampton**, by wards (250), some
fading. 3 ms. [157/425].

Imposition of 5th and 20th on revenue, 1645:
Northampton (town) and **County**. Receipts and
disbursements. By name and hundred only
(3,000+). 72ff. [254/8].

NORTHUMBERLAND

Protestation Returns

Published: *Durham Protestations, or the returns made to the House of Commons in 1641-2 for the maintenance of the protestant religion for the county palatine of Durham, for the borough of Berwick-upon-Tweed and the parish of Morpeth,* ed. H.M. Wood, Surtees Society, vol. **135**, 1922. Indexed

House of Lords Record Office.

Berwick-upon-Tweed (borough and county).
Morpeth Ward: Morpeth (borough).
Both published, above.

No other returns survive for Northumberland.

Note. Taxes raised at this time tended to be at least partially in aid of the northern counties of England, so it is not surprising that there are no records of money raised either from the *Aid to Distressed Protestants in Ireland* or from the *Subsidy* of 1641, which were presumably not levied in these counties.

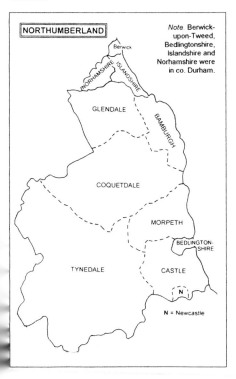

NORTHUMBERLAND

Note. Berwick-upon-Tweed, Bedlingtonshire, Islandshire and Norhamshire were in co. Durham.

GLENDALE

BAMBURGH

COQUETDALE

MORPETH

BEDLINGTON-SHIRE

TYNEDALE

CASTLE

N

N = Newcastle

NOTTINGHAMSHIRE

Parishes: 223.

Protestation Returns (271)

Coverage of the county is good. Over fifty returns have signatures and marks (35 in Bassetlaw Wapentake), indicated by †. Women are mentioned at Carlton in Lindrick and Widmerpool only. Places having lists of clergy and officials only are shown in *italics*.

Published: *Protestation Returns 1641/2 - Nottinghamshire and Derbyshire,* transcribed and published by W.F. Webster, Mapperley, Nottingham, 1980. Arranged alphabetically within each place. Notes on extant parish registers. Lists of clergy etc collated with places. Surname index.

Bassetlaw Wapentake: †(H)Applesthorpe, †Askham, Auckley - *see* Finningley, *Babworth,* Barnby - *see* Hodsock, Beckingham, Bilby - *see* Hodsock, Bilsthorpe, Blyth(e) (*see also* Styrupp), †Bole (Bolle), Bonbusk (*see also* Cuckney), Bothamsall - *see* Elkesley, †Boughton (*see also* Walesby), Budby - *see* Edwinstowe, †West Burton (*u.* W), †Carburton (in Edwinstowe), Carlton in Lindrick, †Clar(e)borough, †Cla(y)worth, Clipston (*see* Edwinstowe), Cottham - *see* South Leverton, Creswell Crags - *see also* Cuckney, Cuckney (*see also* Bonbusk, Creswell Crags, Holbeck, Langwith, Norton, Norwood End, Welbeck, Woodhouse Hall), †Darlton Chapel (in Dunham), †East Drayton (*u.* E; *see also* Stokeham), †West Drayton (*u.* W; *see also* East Markham), †Dunham (*see also* Darlton, Ragnall), †Eakring, †Eaton, †Edwinstowe (*incl.* Budby and Clipston; *see also* Carburton, Perlethorpe and Thoresby), †Egmanton, Elkesley (*incl.* Bothamsall), †Everton, Fenton - *see* Sturton-le-Steeple, Finningley cum Auckley, Gamston, *Gringley on the Hill,* †Grove, Habblesthorpe - *see* Applesthorpe, †Harworth, †Hayton, Headon cum Upton, Hodsock (*incl.* Barnby and Bilby), Holbeck (*see also* Cuckney), Kir(k)ton, †Laneham, Langwith (*see also* Cuckney), †Laxton (Lexington) cum Moorhouse, †North Leverton (*u.* N), †South Leverton (*u.* S) (with Cottham), Littleborough, Lound - *see* Sutton, †East Markham (*u.* E) (*see also* West Drayton), †West Markham (*u.* W), Mattersey, Misson (Mysson), †(some) Misterton, Moorhouse - *see* Laxton, Nettleworth - *see* Warsop, Norton and Norwood End - *see also* Cuckney, †Ollerton, Ompton - *see* Wellow, Ordsall, †Perlethorpe (in Edwinstowe), †Ragnall (in Dunham), †Rampton, Ranskill (*incl.* Serlby and Torworth), East Retford (*u.* E), West Retford (*u.* W), Saun(d)by, *Scrooby,* Serlby - *see* Ranskill, Sookholme - *see* Warsop, †Stokeham (*see also* East Drayton), †Sturton (le Steeple) cum Fenton, Styrupp (*see also* Blythe), Sutton cum Lound, †Thoresby (in Edwinstowe), Torworth (*see* Ranskill), †Treswell or Truswell, †Tuxford, Upton - *see* Headon,

Bassetlaw Wapentake ctd.: Walesby - *see also*
Boughton, †Walkeringham, †Warsop *(incl.*
Nettleworth and Sookholme), Welbeck *(see also*
Cuckney), Wellow (Welley) *(incl.* Umpton), †North
Wheatley *(u. N)*, †South Wheatley *(u. S)*;
Woodhouse Hall *(see also* Cuckney), *Worksop.*
Bassetlaw Wapentake, clergy and officials.

Bingham Wapentake: Adbolton - *see* Holme
Pierrepont, Aslockton (Aslacton) *(see also*
Whatton), Barnston(e) *(see also* Langar),
Bassingfield - *see* Holme Pierrepont, Bingham
(parish) *[see also below for separate publication]*,
East Bridgford *(u. E)*, (Upper or Over) Broughton
(Sulney), Car Colston, Colston Basset, Cotgrave,
Cropwell Bishop, Cropwell Butler *(see also*
Tithby), Elton, †Flintham, Granby, Hawk(e)sworth,
Hickling, Holme Pierrepo(i)nt *(incl.* Adbolton in
Bassingfield), Kinoulton (Knolton), Kneeton,
Langar *(see also* Barnstone), Orston *(see also*
Scarrington, Staunton, Thoroton), Over Broughton
- see Broughton, †Owthorpe, Radcliffe on Trent,
Scarrington (Skerington) *(see also* Orston),
Shelford, †Staunton Chapelry *(see also* Orston),
Thoroton (Thorroughton) *(see also* Orston), Tithby
(see also Cropwell Butler), Tollerton, Whatton
(see also Aslockton).

Broxtow(e) Wapentake: Adenborough - *see*
Attenborough, Annesley (Ansley), Arnold,
Attenborough (Adenborough) *(see also* Bramcote,
Chilwell, and Toton), Babbington Moor - *see*
Greasley, Basford, Beauvale - *see* Greasley,
†(some) Beeston, Bilborough *(see also* Wollaton),
Bramcote *(see also* Attenborough), Brinsley - *see*
Greasley, Bulwell, Chilwell *(see also* Atten-
borough), Cossall, Eastwood, Greasley (Greaslie)
(incl. or see also Babbington Moor, Beauvale,
Beggarlee, Brinsley, Hempshill Hall, Kimberley,
Moor Green, Newthorpe, Watnall Cantelupe and
Watnall Chaworth), Hempshill Hall - *see* Greasley,
Hucknall Torkard, Kimblerley - *see* Greasley,
†Kirkby in Ashfield, Lenton, Linby, Mansfield *(see
also* Skegby), Mansfield Woodhouse, Moor Green
- *see* Greasley, Newstead - *see* Papplewick,
Newthorpe - *see* Greasley, **Nottingham** (town,
incl. high officials and Castle), Nuthall, Papplewick
(incl. Newstead), Radford, Selston, Skegby (in
Mansfield), Stapleford, *Strelley*, Sutton in Ashfield,
Teversall *(see also* Sutton in Ashfield), Toton *(see
also* Bramcote), Trowell, Watnall Cantelupe and
Chaworth - *see* Greasley, Wollaton *(see also*
Bilborough); *Broxtowe Hd.*, clergy and officials.

Newark Hd.: Balderton *(see also* Cotham), Barnby
(in the Willows), Besthorpe - *see* South Scarle,
Bro(a)dholme *(see also* Thorney), North Clifton *(u.
N)* *(see also* South Clifton, Harby and Spalford),
South Clifton *(u. S)* *(see also* North Clifton), North
Collingham *(u. N)*, South Collingham *(u. S)*,
Cotham *(see also* Balderton), Elston, Exeter
House by Newark *(see* Appendix to *Protestation
Returns: Nottinghamshire ...)*,

Newark Hundred, ctd.: Farndon (Farringdon),
†Flawborough *(incl.* Staunton), Girton - *see* South
Scarle, Harby *(see also* North Clifton), †Hawton
(juxta Newark) *(also list in parish regs)*, Kilvington,
Langford, South Scarle, Shelton, Sibthorpe,
Spalford (Spandford) *(see also* North Clifton),
Staunton - *see* Flawborough, Syerston; Thorney
(see also Broadholme and Wigsley); Thorpe (in
the Clotts), Wig(ge)sley *(see also* Broadholme
and Thorney), Winthorpe;
Newark Hd., clergy and officials.

Nottingham (town) - *see* Broxtowe Wapentake.

Rushcliffe Hd.: Barton (in Fabis), Bas(s)ingfield -
see West Bridgford, Bradmore - *see* Bunny,
Bunny (Bonny) *(incl.* Bradmore), West Bridgford
(u. W) *(incl.* Basingfield and Gamston), Clifton
(incl. Glapton), †Costock (Cortlingstock), Edwalton
(in Ruddington), Gamston - *see* West Bridgford,
Glapton - *see* Clifton, Gotham, Keyworth,
†Kingston on Soar, East *(u. E)* and West *(u. W)*
Leake, Normanton upon Soar, Normanton on the
Wolds - *see* Plumtree, Plumtree *(incl.* Normanton
on the Wolds), Ratcliffe (Radcliffe) on Soar,
Rempston(e), Ruddington, †Stanford (on Soar),
Stanton on the Wolds, Sutton Bon(n)ington,
†(some) Thrumpton, †(some) Widmerpool,
Wilford, Willoughby (on the Wolds), Wysall;
Rushcliffe Hd., clergy and officials.

Thurgarton Hd.: Averham, Bathley (Batley) (in
North Muskham), †Bleasby, Blidworth, Burton
Joyce, Calverton, Caunton, †Colwick, Cromwell,
†Edingley, Ep(p)erston(e), Farn(e)sfield,
Fiskerton, Fledborough (Fledburgh), Gedling,
Gonal(d)ston, Gresthorpe - *see* Normanton,
Halam, Halloughton, Hockerton *(see also u.*
Stockerton), Holme, Hoveringham, Kelham,
Kirklington (Kirtlington), Kneesall, Lambley
(Lomly), Lowdham, *Maplebeck*, Marnham (High
and Low), †Morton, North Muskham *(u. N)* (see
also Bathley), South Muskham *(u. S)*, Normanton
(on Trent), Norwell, *Ossington*, Oxton, Rolleston,
†Scrooby, Sne(i)nton, Southwell, Stockerton - *see*
Hockerton, (East) Stoke, *Sutton-on-Trent*,
Thurgarton, Upton, Weston, Winkb(o)urn,
Woodborough;
Thurgarton Hd., clergy and officials.

*Published: Bingham in the Past: Aspects of the
History of a Small Nottinghamshire Town, 1586 to
1780,* by Elizabeth Foster, 1982. Appendix 1.

House of Lords Record Office.

Returns as published, above.

Nottinghamshire Archives, *Nottingham.*

Newark Hd.: Hawton, in parish register.
Microfilm of all returns, as published above
(formerly at *Nottingham Central Library - Local
Studies*).

Nottinghamshire continued.

Taxation Records

Public Record Office [E 179].

Subsidy, 1641:
Wapentakes of **Broxtowe** (30), **Bingham** (?), **Rushcliffe** (100), **Thurgarton** (200). 7 ms. [160/301].
Wapentakes of **Bingham** (130), **Broxtowe** (180), **Rushcliffe** (180), **Thurgarton** (250); some fading. 6 ms. [160/302].
Wapentake of **Bingham** (150), bad in parts. 2 ms. [160/308].
Wapentake of **Rushcliffe** (150), rest (est. 500)
Wapentakes of **Broxtowe, Bingham, Thurgarton;** too difficult. 6 ms. [160/305].
Wapentakes of **Newark** and **Bassetlaw** (450); bad in parts. 4 ms. [160/306].
Wapentakes of **Newark** (200), some fading; **Bassetlaw** (450). 5 ms. [160/304].
Nottingham (50). 2 ms. [160/307].

Assessment, 1642:
Wapentakes of **Newark** and **Bassetlaw** (est. 4,000); double spaced. 10 ms. [160/303].

There are no returns for Nottinghamshire in the *Collection in Aid of Distressed Protestants in Ireland.*

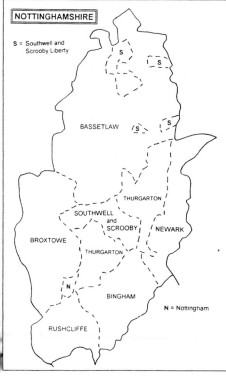

NOTTINGHAMSHIRE

S = Southwell and Scrooby Liberty

BASSETLAW

THURGARTON
SOUTHWELL and SCROOBY
NEWARK
BROXTOWE
THURGARTON

BINGHAM
N = Nottingham

RUSHCLIFFE

OXFORDSHIRE

Parishes: 234.

Protestation Returns (108 + University)

Seven hundreds, in the north-west and extreme south of the county, are extant, approx. 11,800 names. Bullingdon, Dorchester, Ewelme, Lewknor, Pirton, Ploughley and Thame Hds., the city of Oxford and boroughs of Banbury and Woodstock, are missing

Women (**§**) are listed at Asthall, Steeple Barton, and Combe; and at Cokethorpe, Ducklington, Minster Lovell, Southleigh, and Stanton Harcourt are shown in family groups. Six places with signatures and marks are indicated by a dagger (**†**).

Published: *Oxfordshire and North Berkshire Protestation Returns and Tax Assessments 1641-2,* ed. J.S.W. Gibson, Oxon. Record Soc. vol. **59** and Banbury Hist. Soc., vol. **24,** 1994. Indexed. This supersedes Oxon. Record Soc. vol. **36,** 1956 (*Oxfordshire Protestation Returns 1641-2,* ed. C.S.A. Dobson) and the *Index* to vol. 36, by Gwyn de Jong, published by Oxon. F.H.S., 1993.

Bampton Hd.: †Alvescot; §Asthall; Bampton (incl. Weald, Lew, Aston and Cote, Shifford, Chimney, and Brighthampton); Blackbourton; Bradwell; Brize Norton; Broughton Poggs; Burford (including Upton and Signet); Clanfield; §Cokethorpe; Hardwick and Yelford; §Ducklington; Grafton and Radcot; Kelmscott; Kencot; Standlake; Westwell; **Witney;** *Bampton Hundred* (clergy and officials).
Banbury Hd.: Charlbury; †Claydon; Great and Little Bourton; Cropredy; †Mollington; Shutford; Swalcliffe (incl. Sibford Ferris and Sibford Gower); Wardington (incl. Williamscote and Coton).
Binfield Hd.: Caversham; Harpsden; **Henley;** Rotherfield Greys; Rotherfield Peppard; Sonning.
Bloxham Hd.: Adderbury East; Adderbury West; Alkerton; Barford St. John; Bloxham; Bodicote; Broughton (including North Newington); Drayton; Hanwell; Horley; Hornton; Milcombe; Milton; Tadmarton; Wigginton; Wroxton and Balscote.
Chadlington Hd.: Ascot-under-Wychwood; Bruern; Chadlington; Chastleton and Brookend **Chipping Norton;** Churchill; Cornwell; Enstone; Fifield Merrymouth; Fulbrook; Hook Norton; Kingham; Leafield; Lyneham; Milton-under-Wychwood; §Minster Lovell; Northmoor; Over Norton; Ramsden; Great Rollright; Salford; Shipton-under-under-Wychwood; Shorthampton, Chilson and Pudlicote; Spelsbury; Swinbrook; Taynton.
Langtree Hd.: Goring; Ipsden *[clergy and officials only];* Mongewell; Newnham Murren; †North Stoke.
Ploughley Hd.: Although there are no returns for this hundred, Caversfield, a Bucks. enclave belonging to Buckingham Hd., is extant and is published in this volume.

Wootton Hd.: North Aston; †Steeple Aston and †Middle Aston; Barford St. Michael; §Steeple Barton; Westcott Barton; Begbroke; Cassington and Worton; Cogges; Deddington; Duns Tew; Glympton; Heythrop; Kiddington; Kidlington; Northleigh (including Wilcote); §Southleigh; §(Long) Combe; South Newington; Rousham; Sandford St. Martin and Ledwell; Shipton-upon-Cherwell; Stonesfield; §Stanton Harcourt and Sutton; Tackley; Great Tew and Little Tew; Wolvercote; Wootton; Nether Worton; Over Worton; Yarnton (Eardington).

Recusants (all preceding Hundreds).

University of Oxford: Christ Church; Merton College; Magdalen College; New College; Brasenose College; The Queen's College; University College; Corpus Christi College; St. Edmund Hall; Magdalen Hall; Pembroke College; Gloucester Hall; Balliol College; New Inn Hall; St. John's College; Exeter College; Oriel College; All Souls College; Wadham College; Jesus College; St. Mary's Hall; Trinity College; Lincoln College; Alban Hall; Hart Hall.

House of Lords Record Office.

Returns as published, above (except for Caversham).

Berkshire Record Office, *Reading.*

Binfield Hd.: Caversham (formerly Oxon., now in Berkshire), in parish registers, published in Oxon. Record Soc. **59**.

Taxation Records

Published: *Assessment, 1642. Oxfordshire and North Berkshire Protestation Returns and Tax Assessments 1641-42,* as above. This covers:

Bampton Hd.: places as shown under *Protestation Returns,* excl. Burford etc., decayed (577 + many illegible names).

Banbury Hd.: places as *Protestation Returns,* with the addition of Banbury borough and parish (810 names).

Bloxham Hd.: places as *Protestation Returns* (669 names).

Ploughley Hd., North Division (517 names): Ardley; Boycott; Bucknell; Cottisford; Finmere; Fringford; Fritwell; Godington; Hardwick; Hethe; Launton; Lillingstone Lovell; Mixbury and Fulwell; Newton Purcell; Somerton; Souldern; Stoke Lyne; Shelswell; Stratton Audley; Tusmore; Woolaston or Willaston.

Ploughley Hd., South Division (707): Bicester: Market End; Bicester: Kings End; Bletchingdon; Charlton on Otmoor; Chesterton; Hampton Gay; Hampton Poyle; Lower Heyford; Upper Heyford; Islip; Kirtlington; Middleton Stoney; Noke; Oddington; Wendlebury; Weston on the Green. *Recusants.*

Published continued: *Assessment, 1647* (24 June), City of Oxford [P.R.O. E.179/164/499], *Surveys and Tokens,* 'Subsidies and Taxes', ed. H.E. Salter, Oxford Historical Society, vol. **75** (1923), pp. 163-182; 741 names; indexed.

Public Record Office [E 179].

Subsidy, 1641:

Oxford City. South West Ward (60), North West Ward (25), Northgate Ward (80), Southgate Ward (75), Suburbs (70). 2 ms. (3' x 3') [164/477].

Oxford City by wards: North East (80), North West (40), South East (80), South West (40), Suburbs (60). 2 ms. [164/495].

Bampton Hd. (300). 3 ms. [164/487].

Bampton Hd. (100), poor. 2 ms. [164/488].

Bampton Hd. (certificate of default) (8 names). 1 m. [255/1].

Banbury Hd. (130).1 m. [164/508].

Banbury (120) and **Bloxham** (150) **Hds.** 2 ms. [164/481].

Bloxham Hd. (160). 1 m. [164/492].

Bullingdo (300), **Thame** (120) and **Dorchester** (130) **Hds.** 2 ms. [164/478].

Bullingdon (340), **Thame** (150), and **Dorchester** (130) **Hds.** 7 ms. [164/482].

Chadlington Hd. (150); poor. 3 ms. [164/480].

Chadlington Hd. (250), poor in places. 4 ms. [164/485].

Henley with **Lewknor** (150); **Pirton** (80); **Langtree** (90); **Binfield** (150), some poor; and **Ewelme** (230) **Hds.**. 5 ms. [164/483].

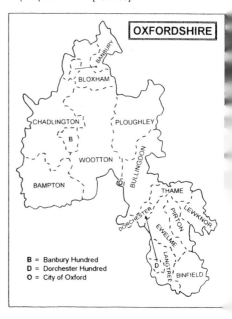

OXFORDSHIRE

B = Banbury Hundred
D = Dorchester Hundred
O = City of Oxford

Oxfordshire: *Subsidy, 1641,* continued

Ploughley Hd. (350), poor. 5 ms. [164/484].
Ploughley Hd. (280). 4 ms. [164/486].
Ploughley Hd. (500), poor in places. 5 ms.
[164/496].
Wootton Hd. (380). 7 ms. [164/479].
Wootton Hd. (400); poor - top missing. 5 ms.
[164/491].
Wootton Hd. (400). 6 ms. [164/494].

Assessment, 1642:
Bampton Hd. (577+); part decayed, repaired.
12 ms. [238/146]. *Published.*
Bloxham and **Banbury Hds.** (1,479). 9 ms.
[164/493]. *Published.*
Ploughley Hd. (1,224). 9 ms. [164/496a]. *Published.*

Parliamentary Assessment, 1647-48:
1647. Bullingdon (943), **Thame** (445) and
Dorchester (237) **Hds.** [164/497]; 6 ms.;
transcript in progress for eventual publication.
1647. Oxford (605) 4 ms. [164/498].
1648. Oxford (741) 4 ms. [164/499]. *Published.*

There are no returns for Oxfordshire in the
Collection in Aid of Distressed Protestants in Ireland.

RUTLAND

Parishes: 50.

Collection in Aid of Protestants in Ireland (21)

Public Record Office [SP 28/194 part 1].

Alstoe Hd.: Teigh.
Martinsley Hd.: Ayston, Clipsham, Edith Weston,
Hambleton, Lyndon [Linden], Manton, Normanton,
Preston Ridlington, Uppingham, Wing.
Wrandike Hd.: Barrowden, Bisbrooke, Caldecott,
Liddington, North and South Luffenham, Pilton,
Stoke Dry, Tixover.

Taxation Records

Public Record Office [E 179].

Subsidy, 1641:
Hds. of **Alstoe** (100); **Oakham Soke** (70);
  Martinsley (80); **Wrandike** (150), poor. [165/190].
Hds. of **Alstoe** (100), fading; **Oakham Soke** (80);
  Martinsley (90); **Wrandike** (140). 5 ms. [165/192].
Hds. of **Alstoe** (100); **Oakham Soke** (100);
  Martinsley (80); **Wrandike** (100), poor in places;
  East (60). 5 ms. [165/193].

There are no *Protestation Returns* for Rutland at
the *House of Lords Record Office.*

SHROPSHIRE

Parishes: 229.

Shropshire continued

Protestation Returns (12)

House of Lords Record Office.

Places duplicated in the *Collection in Aid of Distressed Protestants in Ireland* are asterisked.

Bridgnorth borough (Stottesden Hd.).
Wenlock Franchise/Liberty: *Badger, Barrow, *Beckbury, Benthall, *Broseley, Ditton Priors, Eaton (under Heywood), *Madeley (Market), *Monkhopton, *Little and *Much Wenlock, Willey.
A typed transcript of all these places, by M.A. Faraday, is at the *Society of Genealogists.*

Collection in Aid of Protestants in Ireland (49)

Places duplicated in the *Protestation Returns* are asterisked.

Public Record Office [SP 28/194 part 4 except when shown otherwise].

North Bradford Hd. (Drayton Div.): Adderley, Cheswardine, Drayton in Hales [Market Drayton], Moreton Say, Norton in Hales, Stoke on Tern, Weston (under Redcastle).
South Bradford Hd. (Wellington Div.): Atcham, Buildwas, Great Dawley, Eaton Constantine, [High] Ercall (Magna), Eyton on the Wild Moors, Leighton, Preston on the Wild Moors, Stirchley, Uffington, Great Upton [Magna], Upton Waters, Wombridge [Wambridge], Wellington, Wrockwardine [Rochwardine], Wroxeter.
Brimstree Hd.: Bobbington.
Pimhill Hd.: Fitz, Middle.
Shrewsbury Liberty: Battle(s)field, Grinshill, Great Hanwood, Preston Gubbals [Gobalds]; **Shrewsbury:** St. Chad, St. Julian, St. Mary.
Wenlock Liberty [all in E 179/167/213]: *Badger, *Beckbury, *Broseley, Hughly, *Madeley (Market), Stoke (St.) Milborough, *Monkhopton, Shipton, *Little Wenlock, Much Wenlock.

Unidentified: Kinton [SP 28/194 part 1], Perthenhedery, Sparsbury; 3 un-named.

Taxation Records

Public Record Office [E 179].

Subsidy, 1641:
North Bradford Hd. (250), poor in places. 2 ms. [167/207].
South Bradford Hd. (250), poor. 2 ms. [167/208].
South Bradford Hd. (200). 2 ms. [167/209].
South Bradford Hd. (140). 2 ms. [167/212].
Chirbury Hd. (70), poor in places. 1 m. [167/211].
Condover Hd. (75). 2 ms. [167/210].

Birmingham Central Library (Archives Dept.).

Subsidy 1641 (6 April):
Purslow and Clun Hd. Transcript [Fletcher Collection 343.51; original formerly in the collection of the Earl of Powis of Walcot Park, Salop.; the Shropshire records are now at *Shropshire Records and Research, Shrewsbury,* but this particular document has not been identified].

Collection in aid of restoring St. Paul's Cathedral, London, 1634 (16 September):
Purslow and Clun Hd. Transcript [Fletcher Collection 343.39; original not identified].

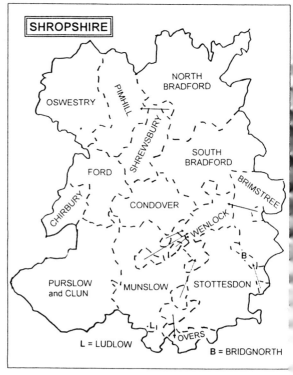

SHROPSHIRE

OSWESTRY · PIMHILL · NORTH BRADFORD · SHREWSBURY · SOUTH BRADFORD · FORD · BRIMSTREE · CHIRBURY · CONDOVER · WENLOCK · PURSLOW and CLUN · MUNSLOW · STOTTESDON · B

L = LUDLOW
OVERS
B = BRIDGNORTH

SOMERSET

Parishes: 486.

Protestation Returns (164)

Returns are extant for places west of a line between Bridgwater and Yeovil (excl. Andersfield, Cannington and North Petherton but incl. Bridgwater); 22,000 names.

Women (§) are named in Buckland St. Mary, Isle Abbots, Hinton St. George, Staple Fitzpaine, Swell, Thurlbear and Winsford. There are signatures and marks (†) in Bridgwater, Culbone, Dodington and West Cranmore; also Winsham (parish register).

Published: The Somerset Protestation Returns and Lay Subsdy Rolls 1641/2, trans. by A.J. Howard, ed. and published by T.L. Stoate, Bristol, 1975. M'fiche edition, £7.00, from Harry Galloway Publications, 39 Nutwell Road, Weston-super-Mare BS22 0EW.

Abdick and Bulstone Hds.: Ashill, Beer Crocombe, Bickenhall [Bicknell], Broadway, §Buckland St. Mary, Cricket Malherbie, Curland, Curry Mallet, Curry Rivell, Drayton, Fivehead, Ilminster and tithings, §Isle Abbots, Isle Brewers, Puckington, §Staple Fitzpaine, Stocklinch Magdalen, §Swell; *Abdick and Bulston Hds.*, clergy and officials - see with South Petherton Hd.; Ilton missing.

Cannington Hd.: Over Stowey - see Williton Freemanors Hd.

Carhampton Hd.: Carhampton (parish), †Culbone (or Kitnor) Cutcombe, Dunster, Exford, Luccombe [Luckham], Luxborough, Minehead, Oare, Porlock, Selworthy, Stoke Pero, Timberscombe, Treborough, Withycombe [Withicombe], Wootton Courtney [Courtenay]; *Carhampton Hd.*, clergy and officials.

Crewkerne Hd.: Crewkerne, §Hinton St. George, Merriott, Misterton, Seaborough; *Crewkerne Hd.*, clergy and officials - see with East Kingsbury Hd.

North Curry Hd.: North Curry (parish), West Hatch, Stoke St. Gregory and hamlets, Thorne Falcon, §Thurlbear; *North Curry Hd.*, clergy and officials.

Glaston(bury) Twelve Hides Hd.: Baltonsborough, West Bradley, Glastonbury St. Benedict and St. John, Meare, West Pennard.

East Kingsbury Hd.: Combe St. Nicholas, Huish (Episcopi), Kingsbury (Episcopi) (parish), East Lambrook, Winsham; *East Kingsbury and Crewkerne Hds.*, Clergy and officials.

West Kingsbury Hd.: Ash Priors, West Buckland, Fitzhead, Ford (Wellington), Bishop's Lydeard [Lydiard Episcopi] and tithings, Wellington (incl. Perry and Woodfords tithings, mis-filed under Bempstone and Williton Hds.), Wiveliscombe; *West Kingsbury Hd.* clergy and officials.

Milverton Hd.: Ashbrittle, Bathealton [Badealton], Kittisford [Kittesford], Langford Budville, Milverton (parish), Runnington [Rownington], Sampford Arundel, Stawley, Thorne St. Margaret; *Milverton Hd.*, clergy and officials.

North Petherton Hd.: †Bridg(e)water.

South Petherton Hd: Barrington, Chillington, Cricket(t) St. Thomas, Cudworth, Dowlish Wake, Knowle (St. Giles), Lopen, South Petherton (parish) and tithings, Seavington (St.) Mary, Seavington (St. Michael with) Dinnington, Shepton Beauchamp, Whitestaunton [Whit Staunton]; *South Petherton, Abdick and Bulston Hds.:* clergy and officials.

Taunton and Taunton Dean Hd.: Angersleigh, (West) Bagborough, Bradford, Cheddon (Fitzpaine), Combe Florey, Corfe, Cothelstone, Heathfield, Hill Farrance, Bishop's Hull (or Hill Bishop), Kingston St. Mary juxta Taunton, Lydeard [Lydiard] St. Lawrence, Norton Fitzwarren, Nynehead [Ninehead], Oake, Orchard (Portman), Otterford, Pitminster [Pitmister], Ruishton [Ryston], Staplegrove, Stoke St. Mary, Taunton, Trull, Wilton, Withiel (Florey); *Taunton Dean Hd.*, clergy and officials; Rimpton and Tollard missing.

Wells Forum Hd.: Binegar, Dinder, Evercreech with Chesterblade, Litton, Priddy, Wells (St. Andrew, Cathedral), Wells (St. Cuthbert), Westbury, Wookey [Wookie].

Whitstone Hd.: Batcombe, †West Cranmore, Croscombe, Ditcheat (with Allhampton and Sutton), Hornblotton, Lamyat(t), Lottisham, East Pennard, Pilton and tithings, Pylle (alias Pull), Shepton Mallet (formerly unidentified), North Wootton, Wraxhall.

Williton and Freemanors Hd.: Bicknoller, Brompton Ralph, Brompton Regis, Brushford, Chipstable, Clatworthy, Old Cleeve, Cro(w)combe, †Dodington, Dulverton, Elworthy, Exton, Halse, Hawkridge, Huish Champflower, Kilton, Kilve, Lilstock, Monksilver, Nettlecombe, East and West Quantoxhead, Raddington, Sampford Brett, Skilgate, Stogumber, Nether Stowey, Over Stowey [in Cannington Hd., but incl. with this Hd.], Upton, Watchet (St. Decumans), §Winsford, Withypoole; *Williton and Freemanors Hd.*, clergy and officials.

House of Lords Record Office.

Returns as published, above.

Somerset Record Office, Taunton.

East Kingsbury Hd.: †Winsham [copy in parish register, D/P/Winsh. 2/1/2].

Collection in Aid of Protestants in Ireland (8)

Public Record Office [SP 28/194 part 4].

Bath Forum Hd.: Bathford, Bathwick, Freshford, **Frome Hd.:** Beckington, Berkley, Frome-Selwood, Road.
Unidentified: West Keinton.

Somerset continued

Petition, 1641

Published: *A Somerset Petition of [15 December] 1641*, transcribed by A.J. Howard. Publication No. SOM/2, March 1968.

This comprises 14,350 persons. Names are arranged alphabetically under each place. No index. Places (where possible) identified from names of clergy and incumbents (but many not identified).

House of Lords Record Office.

Petition, as published, above. Photocopy at *Somerset Record Office.*

Taxation Records

Published: *The Somerset Protestation Returns and Lay Subsdy Rolls 1641/2*, transcribed by A.J. Howard, edited and published by T.L. Stoate, Bristol, 1975. Microfiche edition by Harry Galloway (see above).

The *1641 Subsidy* survives for the whole county [P.R.O. E 179/172/394-5,397-8,400-01,404-07], but for hundreds with an extant *1641 Poll Tax* ('PT') [E 179/172/408] (Bruton, Catash, Horethorne, Norton Ferris) this has been published instead.

The *1642 Assessment* ('A') [E 179/172/409-10] also survives for the hundreds of Carhampton, North Curry, Kingsbury West, Taunton and Williton.

Somerset: *Taxation records* continued

Hundreds are arranged alphabetically. Those for which there are *Protestation Returns* are asterisked.

*Abdick and Bulstone [401], Andersfield [394], City of Bath [404], Bath Forum [398], Bruton [PT 408], *Cannington [394], *Carhampton [397; A 409, and duplicate in E 179/256/6], Catash [PT 408], Chew [407], Chewton [407], *Crewkerne [401], *North Curry [395; A 410], Frome [398], *Glaston Twelve Hides [406], Hartcliffe and Bedminster [405], Horethorne [PT 408], Houndsborough [400], Huntspill and Puriton [394], Keynsham (Keynsham, Chewton, Brislington only, rest illegible) [407], Kilmersdon [398], *Kingsbury East [401], *Kingsbury West [395; A 410], Martock [400], *Milverton [395], Norton Ferris [PT 408], *North Petherton [394], *South Petherton [401], Pitney [400], Portbury [405], Somerton [400], Stone [400], *Taunton [395; A 410], Tintinhull [400], Wellow [398], *Wells Forum [406], Whitley [394], *Whitstone [406], *Williton (and Freemanors) [397; A 409].

Public Record Office [E 179].

Subsidy, 1641 (mostly published, see above):
Hds. of **Abdick and Bulstone** (380), **East Kingsbury** (200), **South Petherton** (200), **Crewkerne** (150); poor. 6 ms. [172/401]. *Pubd.*
Hds. of **Andersfield** (130), **Cannington** (230), **Huntspill and Puriton** (100), **North Petherton** (380), **Whitley** (570). 8 ms. [172/394]. *Published.*

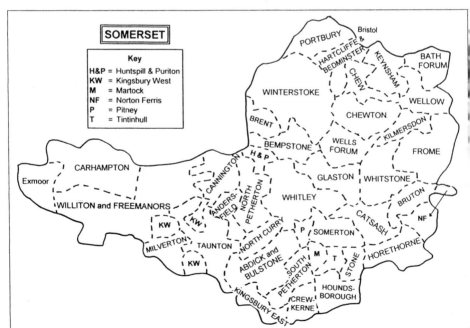

Somerset: *Subsidy, 1641* continued

Hds. of **Andersfield** (100), **Cannington** (150),
  Huntspill and Puriton (50), **North Petherton**
  (300). 5 ms. [172/411].
Bath (130), poor. 1 m. [172/404]. *Published.*
Hds. of **Bath Forum** (100), **Frome** (130),
  Kilmersdon (60), **Wellow** (150), crumbling.
  5 ms. [172/398]. *Published.*
Hds. of **Bath Forum** (130), **Frome** (230), **Wellow**
  (170), **Kilmersdon** (170), poor in places. 6 ms.
  [172/402].
Hds. of **Catsash** (370), **Horethorne** (260), **Bruton**
  (200), **Norton Ferris** (250). 6 ms. [172/396].
Hds. of **Chew** (200), poor; **Chewton** (300);
  Keynsham (250), poor. 6 ms. [172/407]. *Pubd.*
Hds. of **Hartcliffe and Bedminster** (170), **Portbury**
  (180). 2 ms. [172/405]. *Published.*
Hd. and Borough of **Taunton** (580), Hds. of **North**
  Curry (120), **West Kingsbury** (230), **Milverton**
  (140). 8 ms. [172/395]. *Published.*
Hd. and Borough of **Taunton** (600), **North Curry**
  (130), **West Kingsbury** (200), **Milverton** (120); all
  quite poor. 7 ms. [172/399].
Hds. of **Tintinhull** (100), **Houndsborough (Barwick**
  and Coker) (200), **Stone,** (150) **Martock** (120),
  Pitney (40), **Somerton** (160). 4 ms. [172/400].
  Published.
Hds. of **Wells with Wells Forum** (200), **Whitstone**
  (200), **Glaston(bury)** (100); some bad and
  obscure. 8 ms. [172/406]. *Published.*
Hds. of **Williton and Freemanors** (900), some
  gaps; **Carhampton** (450). 10 ms. [172/397].
  Published.

Poll Tax, 1641:
Hds. of **Catsash** (600), **Horethorne** (600), **Bruton**
  (100), **Norton Ferris** (200). 11 ms. [172/408].
  Published.

Assessment, 1642:
Hds. of **Williton and Freemanors** (2,000),
  Carhampton (900), 16 ms. [172/409]. *Published.*
Hd. of **Carhampton**. 13 ms. Duplicate of listing in
  172/409 [256/6].
Borough and Hd. of **Taunton and Taunton Dean**
  (1,250), **North Curry** (1,000), **Milverton** (400),
  West Kingsbury (500). 18 ms. [172/410]. *Pub'd.*

The British Library Manuscripts Collections.

Subsidy, 1641:
Borough of **Bridg(e)water** (100), Hds. of **Whitley**
  (550), **North Petherton** (300), **Cannington** (170),
  Andersfield (80), **Huntspill and Puriton** (370);
  a few lost. 11 ms. [Add. Ch. 28,275]
Hd. of **Taunton and Taunton Dean** with Borough of
  Taunton (550); Hd. of **North Curry** (110); Hd. and
  Borough of **Milverton** (120), faded; and **West**
  Kingsbury (the four Western Tithings) (120).
  7 ms. [Add. Ch. 28,276].
Hd. of **Taunton and Taunton Dean** (370). 3 ms.
  [Add. Ch. 28,277].

Somerset, *British Library, Subsidy 1641* continued

Hds. of **North Curry** (750), **Kingsbury West** (400),
  Milverton (360), **Taunton** (some further local
  locations within parishes) (100), Borough of
  Taunton (with street names) (150). [Add. Ch.
  28,278].

See also 'A by-path of the Civil War', H. Symonds,
Somersetshire Archaeological and Natural History
Society proceedings, **65**(2) (1919), pp. 48-75. Lists
inhabitants of South Brent, Berrow, Burnham, and
Lympsham, who were plundered; also includes
certificates subscribed by many inhabitants of East
Brent, Burnham, Berrow, and South Brent, 1645.

STAFFORDSHIRE

Parishes: 183.

Protestation Returns (58)

House of Lords Record Office.

Effectively returns are only extant for the eastern hundred of Offlow, around Lichfield.

There are signatures and marks (†) on returns for Farwell, Handsworth, Hints and Tipton. The return for Great Barr return shows some relationships.

Offlow Hd.: Clergy and officials.

North Offlow Hd.: Alrewas, Fradley, Orgreave, and Edingale [Edinghall]; Barton under Needwood; (King's) Bromley [Regis]; Burton-upon-Trent; Clifton Campville, Haunton, and Harlaston [Harleston]; Hamstall Ridware; Hanbury, Woodend, Draycoat, Stubby Lane, Fauld, and Coton; Lichfield (city) [by streets; Christian names often in Latin]; Lichfield, St. Michael; Mavesyn Ridware; Newborough and Hoarcross; Pipe Ridware; Rolleston and Anslow [Annesley]; Tatenhill, Callingwood, and Dunstall; Thorpe (Constantine); Tutbury; Whittington; Wychnor [Wichnor]; Yoxall.

South Offlow Hd.: Aldridge, Armitage and Handsacre, †Great Barr, West Bromwich, Darlaston, Drayton Basset(t), Elford, †Far(e)well, †Handsworth [Hannesworth], Harborne, †Hints, Longdon, Norton (Canes) (under Cannock) and (Little) Wyrley, Pelsall, Rushall, Shenstone, †Tipton, Wednesbury, We(e)ford, Wiggin(g)ton, Willenhall and Bentley.

North Pirehill Hd.: Newcastle-under-Lyme.

South Pirehill Hd.: Stow(e).

Collection in Aid of Protestants in Ireland (5)

Public Record Office [SP 28/194 part 4].

East Cuttlestone Hd.: Little Saredon (in Shareshill).

Lichfield (city/borough): St. Chad, St. Mary, St. Michael.

North Pirehill Hd.: Hanley (in Stoke-on-Trent).

Taxation Records

Public Record Office [E 179].

Subsidy, **1641:**
City of **Lichfield** (100), one listing. 1 m. [179/313].
Cuttlestone Hd. (400), fading. 4 ms. [179/315].
Offlow Hd. (750). 5 ms. [179/310].
Offlow Hd. (900). 4 ms. [179/312].
Pirehill Hd. (400), fading. 4 ms. [179/311].
Seisdon Hd. (250), poor. 5 ms. [179/314].
Seisdon Hd. (est. 400), bad in places. 6 ms. [179/318].
Totmonslow Hd. (Totmore); too fragile to examine. 1 m. [179/321a].
Totmonslow Hd. (Totmore) (est. 250), bad in places. 3 ms. [179/319].

Staffordshire, *Taxation records* continued

Assessment **1642:**
City of **Lichfield** (200), one list. 1 m. [179/316].
Seisdon Hd. (1,000), very poor in places. 9 ms. [179/308].

Parliamentary assessment, **1647:**
Offlow Hd. By parish (3,000+). 8 sheets of parchment (2' x 2' each); back and front sheets faded [2656/24].

House of Lords Record Office.

Poll Tax certificates
[Parchment Collection, 27 August 1641]
Seisdon Hd.: Constablewicks of Amblecote, Arley, Bilston, Bushbury, Bobbington, Broom(e), Clent, Codsall, Enville, Himley, Kingswinford, Kinver, Moseley, Oken[?], Orton, Patshull, Pattingham, Pendeford, Nether and Over Penn, Pirton and Trescott, Rowley Regis, Sedgley, Tettenhall Clericorum and Regis, Theley[?], Trysall, Wolverhampton, Wombourn, Wrottesley.

See also 'The **Wallsall** *[sic]* **ship money** papers [**1635-37**]', ed. G.P. Mander, in *Wm. Salt Archaeological Society* (later Staffordshire Record Society), *1931* (1933).

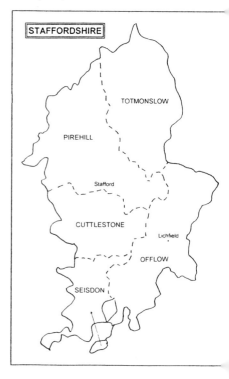

STAFFORDSHIRE

TOTMONSLOW

PIREHILL

Stafford

CUTTLESTONE

Lichfield

OFFLOW

SEISDON

SUFFOLK

Parishes: 532.

Protestation Returns

Published: Leiston, in 'Leiston folk in 1641', *East Anglian Miscellany*, **1931**, pp. 14-15.

Suffolk Record Office, Ipswich.
(* in parish register; † = with signatures and marks.)

*†Friston [FC 124/D2/1; transcript at British Library Additional MSS 41,078], *Harleston [FBA 213/D/1; transcript PRC 140]; †Ipswich St. Stephen [FB 107/A1/1]; *Leiston [FC 130/D/1*], *published*.

No returns for Suffolk at *House of Lords Record Office*.

Vow and Covenant, 1643
Solemn League and Covenant, 1643

Published: Mellis, in 'Solumne League and Covenant in Suffolk', C. Morley, *E.A.M.* **1945**, pp. 30-36.

Suffolk Record Office, Ipswich (except Chilton).
(* in parish register; † = with signatures and marks; Brantham is *Vow* ; all others are *Solemn League*)

*†Brantham [FB 190/D1/1; transcript PRC 527]; *†Brundish [FC 898/A1/1]; *Chilton [*Bury Office:* FL 551/4/1];†Cretingham [FB 51/A1/1]; *†Linstead Parva [FC 193/D1/1; transcript PRC 596]; Mellis [FB 123/A3/1], *published*.

Suffolk continued

Taxation Records

Published: 'Subsidy roll, Suffolk: 15 Car I, Hundred of Lackford and Half Hundred of Exning', Edgar Powell, *East Anglian* N.S. **3** (1890), pp. 241-44, **4** (1891-2), pp. 170-71. This may be from P.R.O. E 179/183/509.
Aldeburgh Poll Tax, 1641, A.T. Winn, Colchester, 1926. Full transcript. This might be from the 1642 Assessment, P.R.O. E 179/183/536.

Public Record Office [E 179].

Subsidy, 1641:
Town of **Aldeburgh** (25). 2 ms. [183/516].
Blackbourn Hd. (?) (230). 5 ms. [183/507]. Dated **1639**.
Hds. of **Blackbourn** (200), some poor; **Thedwestry** (100), poor. 4 ms. [183/512].
Blackbourn Hd. (400). 5 ms. [183/532].
Thedwestry Hd. (150). 3 ms. [183/519].
Blything Hd. (300), poor in parts. 3 ms. [183/534].
Bury St. Edmunds, by wards (200). 2 ms. [183/518].
Hartismere Hd. (250). 3 ms. [183/513].
Hartismere Hd. (500), some fading. 5 ms. [183/531].
Hoxne Hd. (500); a few gaps. 4 ms. [183/511].
Borough of **Ipswich**, by wards (350); poor. 3 ms. [183/510].
Town of **Ipswich**, by wards (270). 3 ms. [183/521].

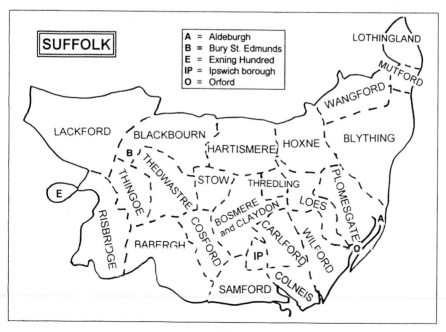

SUFFOLK

A = Aldeburgh
B = Bury St. Edmunds
E = Exning Hundred
IP = Ipswich borough
O = Orford

LOTHINGLAND
MUTFORD
WANGFORD
LACKFORD
BLACKBOURN
HARTISMERE
HOXNE
BLYTHING
B
THEDWASTRE
STOW
THREDLING
E
THINGOE
BOSMERE and CLAYDON
LOES
PLOMESGATE
RISBRIDGE
COSFORD
CARLFORD
WILFORD
A
BABERGH
IP
O
COLNEIS
SAMFORD

Suffolk: *Subsidy,* **1641** continued

Lackford (and Exning) Hds. (150). 1 m. [183/509]. Dated **1639.** *Published?*

Hds. of **Loes** (200), some poor; **Plomesgate** (120); **Colneis** (100), some poor; **Carlford** (120); **Wilford** (100). 5 ms. [183/529].

Town of **Orford** (10). 2 ms. [183/517].

Risbridge Hd. (300). 3 ms. [183/514].

Hds. of **Stow** (est. 100), illegible; **Bosmere and Claydon** (250), poor; **Samford** (100), all poor. 4 ms. [183/520].

Hds. of **Thingoe** (100), **Lackford** (100). 3 ms. [183/515].

Hds. of **Thingoe** (150), **Lackford** (130); poor. 4 ms. [183/549].

Hd. of **Wangford** (150), poor in parts. 3 ms. [183/533].

Assessment, **1642**:

Town and Borough of **Aldeburgh** (400). 2 ms. [183/530] (this might be the published 'Poll Tax').

Town and Borough of **Aldeburgh** (200), some poor. 3 ms. [183/523].

Town and Borough of **Aldeburgh** (200). 3 ms. [183/524].

Blackbourn Hd. (1,600). 9 ms. [183/526].

Blackbourn Hd. (1,300). 10 ms. [183/535].

Borough of **Ipswich** by parishes:
St. Clement (540), St. Helen (100), St. Lawrence (140), St. Margaret (350), St. Mary at the Tower (160), St. Mary atte Church (90), St. Mary Stoke (100), St. Matthew (220), St. Nicholas (220), St. Peter (200), St. Stephen (100); and three hamlets (200). 12 ms. [183/525].

Samford Hd. (2,500). 14 ms. [183/588].

Thedwestry/Thedwastre Hd. (1,200). 6 ms. [183/528].

Wangford Hd. (1,200). 8 ms. [183/522].

See also 'List of subscriptions to the engagement of **1651**', J.J. Raven, *New England historical and genealogical register,* **44** (1890), pp. 365-66. Names for Dennington, Suffolk.

There are no returns for Suffolk in the *Collection in Aid of Distressed Protestants in Ireland.*

SURREY

See *A Guide to Surrey Genealogy and Records,* C. Webb, West Surrey FHS Research Aid **32,** 1991.

Parishes: 146.

Protestation Returns (24)

Returns are extant for the south-east of Surrey only, all places in Reigate and Tandridge Hundreds except for Godstone. Most places have signatures or marks (†). None mention women. Chipstead is written on the back of the printed form.

Places duplicated in the *Collection in Aid of Distressed Protestants in Ireland* are asterisked.

Published: The Surrey Protestation Returns 1641/2, edited by Hector Carter, Surrey Archaeological Society Collections, vol. **59,** pp. 35-68 and 97-104. Guildford, 1962. Indexed.

Reigate Hd.: Betchworth, *†Buckland, †Burstow, *Charlwood, †Chipstead, †Gatton, †Horley, †Leigh, †Merstham, *Nutfield, Reigate (parish).

Tandridge (First Division) Hd.: *†Bletchingley, *†Crowhurst, *†Horne, *†Limpsfield, †Lingfield, *†Oxted, *†Tandridge;
Tandridge Hd., clergy and officials.

Tandridge (Second Division) Hd.: [†Caterham], *Chelsham, *†Farleigh [Farley], *†Tatsfield, *†Titsey, *Warlingham, †Woldingham.

House of Lords Record Office.

Returns as published, above.

Collection in Aid of Protestants in Ireland (61)

Places duplicated in the *Protestation Returns* are asterisked.

Published.

Published: The Relief of Irish Protestants Rolls: Surrey 1642, ed. C.R. Webb, Microfiche, East Surrey FHS R.P. **25** and West Surrey FHS (Microfiche) Series **2,** 1988.

The following places are covered [in P.R.O. SP 28/ 194 part 1 except when shown otherwise]:

Brixton Hd.: Barnes, Lambeth, Merton [SP 28/195], Mortlake, Putney [SP 28/193 filed with Middlesex and London], Tooting, Wandsworth.

Copthorne Hd.: Ashtead, Banstead, Chessington, Fetcham [E 179/187/47], Mickleham [E 179/257/ 25], Newdigate.

Effingham Hd.: Great and Little Bookham, Effingham.

Elmbridge Hd.: Cobham, Esher, Stoke D'Abernon [SP 28/194 part 2], Walton on Thames, Weybridge.

Farnham Hd.: Elstead, Farnham, Seale.

Godalming Hd.: Chiddingfold, Haslemere [E 179/257/24], Thursley [E 179/257/26], Witley [E 179/ 257/24].

Godley Hd.: Chertsey [E 179/257/26], Egham, Thorpe.

Surrey: *Collection,* continued

Kingston Hd.: Long Ditton, Thames Ditton, Kingston (on Thames), Maldon, Petersham.

Reigate Hd.: *Buckland, *Charlwood, Kingswood, *Nutfield.

Tandridge Hd.: *Bletchingley, *Chelsham, *Crowhurst, *Farleigh, Godstone, *Horne, *Limpsfield, *Oxted, *Tandridge, *Tatsfield, *Titsey, *Warlingham [E 179/ 257/25].

Wallington Hd.: Chaldon, Coulsdon, Croydon Sanderstead, Sutton, Woodmansterne.

Wotton Hd.: Dorking.

Public Record Office.

Returns as published, above.

Taxation Records

Published: Calendar of Lay Subsidies: Western Surrey, 1603-1649, compiled by Cliff Webb, West Surrey F.H.S. Record Series, vol. 4, 1984. Indexed. The relevant part of this is a transcript of the **1641 Subsidy** [E 179/186/451, collated with E 179/187/466 and E 179/186/461].

Surrey: *Taxation records* continued

Places covered are:

Blackheath Hd.: Albury, Alfold, Bramley, Cranleigh, Dunsfold, Ewhurst, Hascombe, St. Martha's (two names only), Shalford, Shere, Wonersh.

Farnham Hd.: Badshot, Churt, Elstead, Farnham, Frensham, Runfold, Runwick, Seale and Tongham, Tilford, Waverley (one name only), Wrecclesham.

Godalming Hd.: Artington and Littleton (in St. Nicholas Guildford), Binscombe, Cattershall, Chiddingfold, Compton, Eashing, Farncombe, Godalming, Hambledon, Haslemere, Hurstmore [Hurting], Peperharow, Shackleford, Thursley, The Weald, Witley.

Godley Hd.: Bisley, Byfleet [Bislett], Chertsey, Chobham, Egham, Frimley, Pyrford, Thorpe.

Woking Hd.: Ash, East and West Clandon, Guildford, East and West Horsley, Merrow, Ockham (with) Wisley, Pirbright, Send and Ripley, Stoke (next Guildford), Wanborough (one name only), Windlesham and Bagshot, Woking, Worplesdon.

Wotton Hd.: Abinger, Capel, Dorking, Ockley, Wotton (parish).

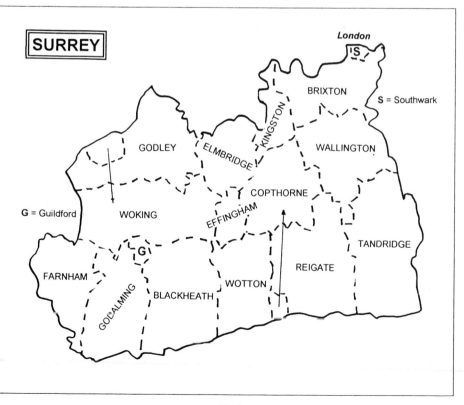

69

Surrey: *Taxation records* continued

Public Record Office [E 179].

Subsidy, 1641:
Brixton Hd. (600). 3 ms. [186/448].
Guildford and Hds. of **Farnham** (170), **Godalming**, (220), **Godley** (230), **Blackheath** (200), **Woking** (350), **Wotton** (120) 29 ms. [186/451]. *Published.*
Southwark (St. Saviour) (200). 2 ms. [186/452].
Wallington Hd. (160). 2 ms. [186/453]. Transcript for publication by WS FHS.
Brixton Hd. (400), some poor. 4 ms. [186/454].
Southwark (St. Olave), Landside and Waterside and aliens. (330). 2 ms. [186/455].
Southwark (St. George), illegible. 1 m. [186/456].
Southwark (St. Olave), Landside and Waterside and aliens (300), some poor. 2 ms. [186/457].
Southwark (St. George) (100). 2 ms. [186/458].
Southwark (St. Saviour) (260). 2 ms. [186/459].
Hds. of **Woking, Wotton, Farnham, Godalming, Godley** and **Blackheath**; mostly illegible. 8 ms. [187/461]. *Published.*
Wallington Hd. (200), poor. 2 ms. [187/464]. Transcript for publication by WS FHS.
Brixton Hd. (500), some gaps. 3 ms. [187/465].
Guildford and Hds. of **Farnham, Goldalming, Godley, Blackheath, Woking** and **Wotton**; too fragile to examine. 8 ms. [187/466]. *Published.*
Brixton Hd. (certificates of defaulters), very difficult. 12 ms. [257/27], dated **1642**.
Southwark (St. Thomas) (300). 1 m. [187/474].

Assessment Poll Tax, 1641:
Southwark (St. Saviour), locations within parish (600). 5 ms. [257/22].
Southwark (St. Olave), rather poor in places (est. only 400). 5 ms. [257/23].

Assessment, 1642:
Liberty of the **Clink** (450) and the Parish Garden (Southwark) (120). 2 ms. [187/469].
Southwark (St. Olave) (400), Landside and Waterside,very mutilated; (St. Saviour) (600), mentions streets, alleys, yards etc. by name. 6 ms. [187/470].
Reigate Hd. (500), some poor. 6 ms. [187/463].
Southwark (with certificate of defaulters) (450). 5 ms. [186/447].
Southwark (defaulters) (60). 1 m. [186/449], dated **1643**.
Southwark (St. Olave) (200), some gaps. 1 m. [186/450], dated **1644**.

Guildford Muniment Room, Surrey R.O.

1640/1, 1649, 1650. Subsidy lists (transcripts from Public Records) [Bray papers: 85/2/8(1) pp. 262-305].

SUSSEX

Parishes: 305.

Protestation Returns (158)

Returns for the Rapes of Arundel, Bramber, and Chichester, which comprise West Sussex, are almost complete (missing include Arundel, South Bersted, Bosham, Bramber, Linch, New Shoreham). There are signatures and marks (†) at 28 places. West Dean shows family groups. However, women are not mentioned in any returns. That for Tangmere is on the back of the printed Protestation form.

The only returns extant for East Sussex are found in parish registers.

Published: West Sussex Protestation Returns, *1641-2,* edited by R. Garraway Rice, Sussex Record Society, vol. **5**, 1906. 12,819 names. Indexed (surnames only).
East Sussex: Sussex Family Historian, vol. **2**, pp. 84-89, Brighton, 1975. From parish registers:
Hastings Rape: Whatlington.
Pevensey Rape: Alfriston, Ringmer.

Places in West Sussex for which returns (as published in S.R.O. **5**) are duplicated in the *Collection in Aid of Distressed Protestants* are asterisked.

Arundel Rape
Clergy and officials.
Avisford Hd.: *Barnham, Binstead, *Climping, *Eastergate, *Felpham, Ford(e), Madehurst, *Middleton, *South Stoke, *†Tortington, *Walberton, *Yapton.
Bury Hd.: *Bignor cum Buddington, *Burton cum Coates, Bury (parish), *Coldwaltham, *Fittleworth, Hardham, *Houghton, Loxwood, *Wisborough Green.
Poling Hd.: *Angmering, *Burgham alias Burpham, *Ferring and Kingston, *Goring, *Lyminster [Limister], *Littlehampton, *†Poling (parish), *East Preston, West Preston, *North Stoke, *Warningcamp.
Rotherbridge Hd.: Barlavington, *Duncton [Downcton], Egdean, *Kirdford, *Lurgashall [Lurgushall], *Northchapel, *Petworth, *Stopham, *Sutton, *Tillington, *Woolavington.
West Easwrith Hd.: Amberley, †Billingshurst, *(West) Chiltington, *Parham, Pulborough, *Rudgwick, *Slinfold, Storrington, †*Wigginholt with *Greatham.

Bramber Rape
Brightford Hd.: †Broadwater [part misfiled under Washington], *†Clapham, *†Findon, *†Lancing [Launsing], *Sompting.
Burbeach Hd.: *Edburton [Auburton], *Ifield, *†Seal (or Beeding).
East Easwrith Hd.: *Horsham (borough and parish), *Itchingfield [Hitchingfield], *†Sullington, Thak(e)ham, Warminghurst.

ishergate Hd.: *†Kingston by Sea [Kinson Bonsye], *†Old Shoreham, *†Southwick.

Vest Grinstead Hd.: *†Ashington, *†Ashurst, *West Grinstead, *Shipley.

atching Hd.: *†Patching (parish).

inglecross Hd.: *Nuthurst, *Rusper, *Warnham.

teyning Hd.: *†Botolphs [Buttolphs], *†Coombs [Coomes], *†Steyning (parish), *Washington, *†Wiston

arring Hd.: *†(West) Tarring (parish).

ipnoak Hd.: *†Albourn and *Woodmancote, *†Henfield.

Vindham and Ewhurst Hd.: *Cowfold, Shermanbury.

Chichester Rape

lergy and officials.

Idwick Hd.: East Lavant, *Pagham, Slindon, *Tangmere [on back of form].

osham Hd.: Funtington, West Stoke, West Thorney.

ox and Stockbridge Hd.: Aldingbourne [Alinbourne], †Appledram, Boxgrove; Chichester: Cathedral Close, St. Bartholomew without the West Gate, St. Pancras without the liberty of the City, St. Pancras within the liberty of the City, St. Andrew, All Saints within the city, St. Martin, St. Olave, St. Peter the Great, St. Peter the Less, Chichester city officials; Donnington, Eartham, New Fishbourne, Hunston, Merston, North Mundham, †Oving, †Rumboldswyke, Upwaltham, Westhampnett.

umpford Hd.: *Chithurst, *Elstead, *Rogate, *Treyford [Trayford] cum Didling, *†Trotton, Turwick.

asebourne Hd.: *Bepton, *Cocking, *†Easebourne [Eastbourn] (parish), *Fernhurst [Farnhurst], *Graffham, *Heyshott, *Iping, *Linchmere, *Lodsworth, *Midhurst, *†Selham, *Stedham, *Woolbeding; one place unidentified.

anhood Hd.: *Birdham, Earnley, (West) Itchenor, Selsey, Sidlesham, East Wittering, *West Wittering.

estbourne and Singleton Hds.: *Binderton, *Compton cum *Upmarden, East Dean, *West Dean, Chilgrove and Stapleash, *East Mardon, North Marden, *Mid Lavant, Racton, *Singleton (parish), *Stoughton, *Westbourne (parish); two unidentified places.

ouse of Lords Record Office.

Returns as published in S.R.O. 6, above.

st Sussex Record Office, Lewes

Returns in parish registers as published in *Sussex mily Historian,* above, plus Wilmington (Pevensey pe).

Collection in Aid of Protestants in Ireland (168)

Places in West Sussex for which *Protestation Returns* (as published in S.R.O. 6) are duplicated in the *Collection in Aid of Distressed Protestants* are asterisked.

Published: *East Sussex Contributors to the Relief of Irish Protestants 1642,* compiled by M.J. Burchall, Sussex Genealogical Centre, Occasional Paper No. 10, 1984. Not indexed. This includes all places in the Rapes of **Hastings, Lewes** and **Pevensey** listed below, and Ifield in the Rape of Bramber.

[*Public Record Office,* all in C 179/191/390 except for those shown as being in SP 28/194 part 4].

West Sussex:

Arundel Rape *(Avisford, Bury, West Easwrith, Poling, Rotherbridge Hds.):* *Angmering, Arundel, *Barnham, *Bignor, *Burpham [Burgham alias], Burton, *Burton cum Coates, *North Chapel, *(West) Chiltington [SP 28/194/4], *Climping, Coates *see* Burton, *Coldwaltham, *Duncton [Downcton], *Eastergate, *Felpham, *Ferring, *Fittleworth, *Goring (by Sea), *Greatham, *Houghton, *Kirdford, Lavington (East and West) *see* Woolavington, *Littlehampton [Little Hampton], *Lurgashall [Lurgushall], *Lyminster [Limister], *Middleton, *Parham [SP 28/194/4], *Petworth, *Poling, *East Preston, *Rudgwick, Rustington, *Slinfold, *North Stoke [Northstock], *South Stoke, *Stopham, *Sutton, *Tillington, *Tortington, *Walberton, *Warningcamp, *Wiggenholt [Wiggonholt, Wigenholt] [SP 28/194/4], *Wisborough Green, *Woolavington [SP 28/194/4], *Yapton.

Bramber Rape *(Brightford, Burbeach, East Easwrith, Fishergate, West Grinstead, Patching, Singlecross, Steyning, Tarring, Tipnoak, Windham and Ewhurst Hds.):* Adburton *see* Edburton, Albourne, *Ashington [SP 28/194/4], *Ashurst [SP 28/194/4], (Upper) *Beeding [Beedmore] alias Sele [Seal] [SP 28/194/4], *Botolphs [Buttolphs], *Clapham [SP 28/ 194/4], *Coom(b)es, *Cowfold, *Edburton [Adburton], *Findon, *West Grinstead [two returns, one in SP 28/194/4], Heene, *Henfield, Hitchingfield *see* Itchingfield, *Horsham, *Ifield, *Itchingfield, *Kingston by Sea [Bowsey], *Lancing [Launsing] [SP 28/194/4], *Nuthurst [SP 28/194/4], *Patching, *Rusper, Sele/Seal *see* Beeding, *Shipley [SP 28/194/4], New Shoreham, *Old Shoreham, Slinfold *see* Arundel Rape, *Sompting, *Southwick, *Steyning [two returns], *Sullington, *(West) Tarring, *Warnham, *Washington, *Wiston, *Woodmancote and Albourne [two returns, one in SP 28/194/4].

Sussex: *Collection (West Sussex)* continued

Chichester Rape *(Aldwick, Bosham, Box and Stockgrove, Dumpford, Easebourne, Manhood, Westbourne and Singleton Hds.)***:** *Bepton, Bersted [SP 28/194/4], *Binderton [SP 28/194/4], *Birdham [SP 28/194/4], Bosham, Chidham, *Chithurst, *Cocking, *Compton [SP 28/194/4], *(West) Dean(e) (with Chilgrove and Stapleast) [SP 28/194/4], *Easebourne [Eastbourn], *Elsted, *Fernhurst [Farnhurst], *Graffham, (South) Harting, *Heyshott, *Iping, *Mid Lavant [SP 28/194/4], *Linchmere [Lynchmore], *Lodsworth, Lordington (in Racton) [SP 28/194/4], *East Marden [SP 28/194/4], *Up Marden [SP 28/194/4], *Midhurst, *Pagham [SP 28/194/4], *Rogate, *Selham, *Singleton [SP 28/194/4], *Stedham, *Stoughton [SP 28/194/4], *Tangmere, Terwick, *Treyford (cum Didling), *Trotton, *Westbourne (incl. Prinsted), *West Wittering [SP 28/194/4], *Woolbeding [Wool Beeding];
three unidentified places (one in Easebourne Hd., two in Westbourne and Singleton Hd.).

East Sussex:
Hastings Rape *(Baldstrow, Battle, Bexhill, Foxearle, Goldspur, Gostrow, Guestling, Hawkesborough, Henhurst, Netherfield, Ninfield, Shoyswell, Staple Hds.)***:** Ashburnham, Beckley, Brightling, Burwash, Crowhurst, Dallington, Etchingham, Ewhurst, Fairlight [Fareleigh], Guestling, East Guldeford, Heathfield, Herstmonceux, Hollington, Hooe [SP 28/194/596], Icklesham, Iden, Mo(u)ntfield, Northiam, Peas(e)marsh, Penhurst, Pett, Playden, Salehurst, Sedlescombe, Udimore [SP 28/194/601], Warbleton, Wartling, Westfield, **Winchelsea** [SP 28/194/4].

Sussex: *Collection (East Sussex),* continued

Lewes Rape *(Barcombe, Buttinghill, Dean, Fishergate, Holmstrow, Poynings, Preston, Street, Swanborough, Whalebone, Younsmere Hds.)***:** Edburton *see* Bramber Rape, Hove, **Lewes** All Saints [SP 28/194/607], Preston by Hove.

Pevensey Rape *(Alciston, Bishopstone, Danehill, Dill, Eastbourne, Flexborough, East Grinstead, Hartfield, Longbridge, Loxfield Dorset, Loxfield Pelham, Pevensey Lowey, Ringmer, Rotherfield, Rushmonden, Shiplake, Totnore, Willingdon Hds.)***:** Alfriston, Arlington, Berwick, Chalvington [Chaunton], Chiddingly [Chittingley] [SP 28/194/594], (East) Dean, West Dean, Denton [SP 28/194/595], (?)Flaxborough [SP 28/194/4], Frant [SP 28/194/634], Friston, Hartfield, East Hoathly, Jevington, Laughton, Litlington, Mayfield, Ripe, Rotherfield [SP 28/ 194/396–41], Wadhurst, Waldron, Willingdon, Wil(l)mington, Withyham [SP 28/194/605].

Unidentified: Hoodham, Whitcham [SP 28/194/4], Worning; one unidentified [SP 28/194/4].

Solemn League and Covenant, 1644

East Sussex Record Office, Lewes:

Pevensey Rape: Newhaven (in parish register). *Published,* Sussex Family Historian, vol. **2**, pp. 84-89, Brighton, 1975.

Taxation Records

Public Record Office.

Assessment:
1642. Rape of **Bramber** (2,000). 11 ms.
[E 179/258/12].

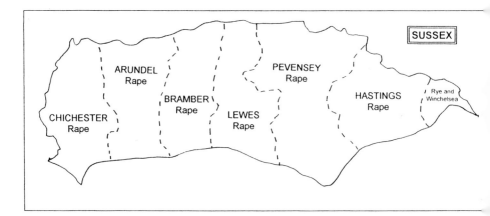

WARWICKSHIRE

Parishes: 208.

Protestation Returns (19)

The only extant returns are for Coventry and vicinity, and a few places in Knightlow Hundred, all to the south and east between Coventry and Southam, except for Arley.

No returns have signatures and marks, and women are not mentioned. The return for Wolfhamcote is on the back of the printed form.

House of Lords Record Office.

Coventry City and County: Anst(e)y, **Coventry** (city), Exhall, Foleshill, (Walsgrave-on-)Sowe, Stivichall, Stoke, Wyken.
Knightlow Hd.: Arley, Harbury, Leamington Hastings and townships, Napton-on-the-Hill, Offchurch, Ryton on Dunsmore, Stoneleigh [Stonely], Wappenbury, Weston under We(a)therly, Wolfhamcote, Wolston.
Microfilm at *Warwick County Record Office.*

Warwickshire continued

Collection in Aid of Protestants in Ireland

Public Record Office [SP 28/136].

Stratford-upon-Avon. This appears to be a stray survival, not amongst the main records of the Collection. Although the photocopy, below, shows the P.R.O. piece number, the actual document has not yet been identified amongst the many under this reference.

One return [P.R.O. SP 28/195] described in the lists as of Honnington, Warwickshire, is considered by Cliff Webb actually to be almost certainly for Hornington, Lincolnshire. There are no other Warwickshire returns (apart from Stratford, above).

Shakespeare Birthplace Trust Record Office, Stratford-upon-Avon:

Stratford-upon-Avon [Photocopy PR 307/6].

Taxation Records

Public Record Office.

Subsidy, 1640/1:
Barlichway Hd. (defaulters) (200) gaps. 5 ms. [E 179/194/320].

Assessment(?), 1648-50:
Coventry. Certificates of defaulters. Each m. is dated differently. Possible duplication of names (1,000+). 10 ms. [194/319].

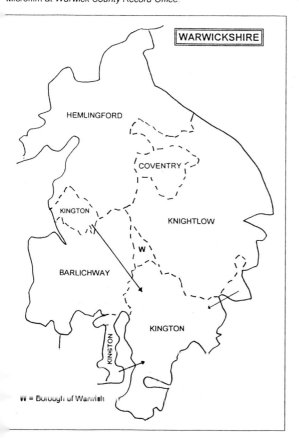

W = Borough of Warwick

73

WESTMORLAND

Parishes: 73.

Protestation Returns (31)

Returns are extant for whole of the north of the county, East Ward and West Ward. There are signatures and marks for eight places, as indicated by a dagger (†).

Published: *The Westmorland Protestation Returns 1641/2*, edited by M.A. Faraday. Cumberland and Westmorland Antiquarian and Archaeological Society Tracts Series, No. **17**. 1971. Indexed.
This includes the whole of both East Ward (2,111) and West Ward (3,378):

East Ward: †Appleby (†St. Lawrence and †St. Michael), Asby, Brough under Stainmore, †Crosby Garrett, Dufton, Kirkby Stephen and townships, Kirkby Thore [Thure], (Long) Marton, Milburn, †Musgrave, Newbiggin [Newbygin] (-on-Lune), †Ormside [Ormeshead], †Orton, Ravenstonedale, Temple Sowerby, Warcop.
West Ward: Askham, Bampton, Barton, Bo(u)lton (nr Appleby), Brougham [Browham], Cliburn [Cleburn], †Clifton (nr Penrith), Crosby Ravensworth, Lowther, Martindale (in Barton), Morland, †Patterdale and Hartsop[p], Shap[p], Thrimby and †Little Strickland.

House of Lords Record Office.

Returns as published, above.

Taxation Records

Public Record Office [E 179].

Subsidy, 1641:
Kendal (barony). Certificate of defaulters. Six only named (five of them women). 1f. [195/70].

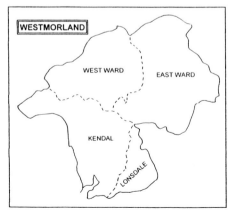

WESTMORLAND

WEST WARD

EAST WARD

KENDAL

LONSDALE

Westmorland: *Taxation records* continued

Cumbria Record Office, *Kendal.*

Subsidy, 1641:
West and East Wards [WD/CAT/MUS/A 2016].

Note. Taxes raised at this time tended to be at least partially in aid of the northern counties of England, so it is not surprising that there are no records of money raised from the *Aid to Distressed Protestants in Ireland*. The only extant *P.R.O.* holding of the *Subsidy* (with names) is of defaulters. The recent discovery of the *1641 Subsidy* now in the *Cumbria R.O.* confirms that this was indeed raised in the county.

WILTSHIRE

Parishes: 318.

Protestation Returns (90)

Returns are extant only for the south-eastern part of the county. These are all listed together in one book, with no signatures and marks. No women are mentioned. Places for which only clergy and officials are listed are in *italics*.

Places duplicated in the *Collection in Aid of Distressed Protestants in Ireland* are asterisked.

Published: 'Wiltshire protestation returns of 1641-2', E.A. Fry, *Wiltshire Notes and Queries*, vol. **7**, 1911-13, pp. 16-21, 79-84, 105-10, 162-7, 203-8, 260-65, 309-13, 343-7, 418-21, 450-52, 496-9.
These are likely to be republished, with an index, by Wiltshire FHS.

Salisbury Division
Alderbury Hd.: *Alderbury and Waddon, West Dean and *Grimstead, Durrington, *Idmiston, *Loverstoke and Ford, *Pitton and Farley, Platford Porton and Gomeldon, *Winterbourne Dauntsey, *Winterbourne Earls, *Winterbourne Gunner, *Winterslow.
Amesbury Hd.: *Allington, Amesbury (parish), *Boscombe, *Brigmerston [Breymaston]*, Bulford, *Cholderton [Chouldrington]*, Great and Little Durnford, *Durrington*, Figheldean, *Ludgershall [Lurgeshall]*, *Milston*, Netton (Durnford), New Town, *Newton Toney, Normington, Salterton, *North Tidworth, *West Wellow.*

Branch and Dole Hd.: *Bemerton, *Berwick St.
James, Burden's Ball [Burthenstall], Chilhampton,
*Fisherton Anger, *Fuggleston St. Peter [Foulstan]
and Quidhampton, (Little) Langford [Parva],
*Steeple Langford, *Mad(d)ington, *South Newton
and Wishford Parva, *Orcheston St. Mary,
*Rollestone, *Sherrington, *Shrewton, *Stapleford,
Stoford [Stowford], *Tilshead, Ugford St. Giles,
Wilton [*Collection under* Wilton **borough**],
*Winterbourne Stoke, *Great Wishford, Wylye.

Cawden and Cadworth Hd.: *Barford St. Martin,
*Baverstock and Hurcott, *Bramshaw, *Britford
and East Harnham, South Burcombe, *Co(o)mbe
Bissett, *Fovant [Foffont], *West Harnham,
*Homington, *Netherhampton [*Collection under*
Wilton borough], *Odstock(e), Stratford Toney
[St. Anthony], *Sutton Mandefield, *Whitsbury
[Whichbury].

Chalk Hd.: Alvediston, Berwick St. John, Bower
Chalk, Broad Chalk, Ebbesbourne, Fifield
(Bavant), Semley, Tollard Royal.

Downton Hd.: Bishopston(e), Bodenham, Downton
(parish), Fallerston, Flambston, Nunton,
Standlynch [Standlinch].

Elstub and Everleigh Hd.: *Collingbourn(e) Ducis,
*En(d)ford, Everleigh (parish), *Fifield, *Fittleton
and Haxton [Hackton], *Ham, *Little Hinton*,
*Netheravon, *East Overton, *Patney; Rollestone
see Branch and Dole Hd., *Stockton*.

Frustfield Hd.: Langford, *White(parish)*.

Underditch Hd.: Heale, Milford, Stratford sub
Castle [Stratford Dean], Stratford Coen, *Wilsford,
Wilsford Lake, *Great and Little Woodford.

Wilton Borough: *see* Branch and Dole, Cawden
and Cadworth Hds.

House of Lords Record Office.

Returns as published, above.

Collection in Aid of Protestants in Ireland (217)

Places duplicated in the *Protestation Returns* are
asterisked.

Public Record Office [SP 28/195 unless stated
otherwise].

Alderbury Hd.: *Alderbury, *West Grimstead,
*Idmiston, *Laverstock, *Pitton and Farley,
*Winterbourne Da(u)ntsey, *Winterbourne Earls,
*Winterbourne Gunner [Garner], *Winterslow.

Amesbury Hd.: *Allington, *Boscombe,
*Cholderton, Hurst (enclave in Berks.), *Newton
Ton(e)y, Swallowfield (enclave in **Berks.**), *(North)
Tidworth, *West Wellow.

Branch and Dole Hd. [all in E 179/259/23]:
*Bemerton, *Berwick St. James, *Fisherton Anger,
*Fugglestone, *Steeple Langford, *Maddington,
*South Newton, *Orcheston St. Mary,
*Roll(e)stone, *Sherrington, *Shrewton,
*Stapleford, *Tilshead, *Winterbourne Stoke,
*Great Wishford. *See also* Wilton Borough.

Cawden and Cadworth Hd.: *Barford (St. Martin),
*Baverstock *Bramshaw [which gave nothing!],
*Britford, *Co(o)mbe Bissett, *Fovant, *West
Harnham, *Homington, *Odstock, *Stratford
Ton(e)y, *Sutton Mandeville, *Whitsbury.

Chippenham Hd.: Bidd(l)estone, Box, Castle
Combe, Chippenham (parish), Corsham, Easton
Grey, Langley Burrel(l), Leigh Delamere, Littleton
Drew, Luckington, [Great] Sherston (Magna),
Sopworth, Tytherton Lucas, North Wraxall
[Wroxall], Yatton Keynell.

Damerham Hd (North and South).: Christian
Malford, Compton Chamberlayne [Chamberlain],
South Damerham (parish), [Deverhill or Deverell]
Longbridge (Deverill), Grittleton, Kington St.
Michael, Martin, Monkton Deverill, Nettleton.

Downton Hd.: Knoyle Episcopi *see* Mere Hd.

Dunworth Hd.: Anst(e)y, Chicklade, Chilmark,
Donhead [Dunhead] St. Andrew and St. Mary,
Fonthill Gifford, Sedg(e)hill, Swallowcliffe, Teffont
Evias [Ewyas], Great Teffont, Tisbury.

Elstub and Everleigh Hd.: Alton (Priors) and
Stowell, *Collingbourn(e) Ducis, *En(d)ford,
*Fittleton, *Fyfield(?, in Endford), *Ham, Little
Hinton, *Netheravon, Overton *see* Selkley Hd.,
*Patney, Rollestone *see* Branch and Dole Hd.,
Stockton, Westwood, Wroughton.

Frustfield Hd.: *Whiteparish.

Heytesbury Hd.: Boyton and Corton, Brixton
Deverill, Chitterne All Saints and St. Mary,
Codford St. Mary and St. Peter, Heytesbury
(parish), Hill Deverill, Horningsham, Imber,
Orcheston St. George, Upton Lovell.

Highworth, Cricklade and Staple Hd.: Ashton
Keynes, Broad Blunsdon, Blunsdon St. Andrew,
Castle Eaton, Cricklade [Crickland] St. Mary and
St. Sampson, Eisey, Hannington, Highworth
(parish), Latton, Leigh in Ashton Keynes, Marston
Meysey [Maisey], South Marston, Poulton, Purton,
Rodbo(u)rne Cheney, Shorncott [Shorncote],
Somerford Keynes, Stanton (Fitzwarren) by
Highworth, Stratton St. Margaret.

Kingsbridge Hd.: Chiseldon, Clyffe Pypard
[Peppard], Hilmarton, Liddington, Lydiard Tregoze
[Treguze], Lyneham, Swindon, Tockenham,
Wanborough, Wootton Bassett.

Kinwardstone Hd.: Great and Little Bedwyn,
Burbage [E 179/28/194/1], Buttermere, Chilton
Foliat, Chute, Collingbourn(e) Kingston(e) [SP
28/194/1], Easton [SP 28/194/1], Froxfield, Milton
(Lilbo(u)rne), Pewsey [SP 28/194/1], Shalbourne,
Tidcombe [Titcombe], Wootton Rivers.

Wiltshire: *Collection* continued

Melksham Hd.: Bulkington (in Keevil), Hilperton, Melksham, Poulshot, Seend, Staverton, Trowbridge, Whaddon.

Mere Hd.: (East) Knoyle [Episcopi], West Knoyle, Maiden Bradley, Mere, Stourton.

Potterne and Cannings Hd.: Bromham, Chittoe, **Devizes** St. John the Baptist and St. Sampson, Highway, (West) Lavington [Episcopi], Potterne, Rowde.

Ramsbury Hd.: Baydon, Bishopston(e), Ramsbury (parish) [E 179/259/24].

Selkley Hd.: Fyfield(?, in Overton), Marlborough St. Peter, *Overton [Prot. Ret. under Elstub Hd.].

Swanborough Hd.: All Cannings, Alton Barnes, Beechingstoke [Beechinestoke] and Botwell, Charlton, [Great and Little] Cheverill (magna and Parva), Etchilhampton, Imber *see* Heytesbury Hd., (East or Market) Lavington [Forum], Manningfield Bruce, Marden, North New(n)ton and Hilcott [Hulcot], Rushall, Stanton St. Bernard, Stert, Upavon, Urchfont, Woodborough.

Underditch Hd.: Laverstock *see* Alderbury Hd., Stratford sub Castle, *Wilsford and Manningford, *Woodford and *Wilsford [E 179/246/6].

Warminster Hd.: Bishopstrow, Corsley, Dinton, [Fenny] Sutton Veny, [Norton] (North) Bavant, [Great] Teffont (Magna), Warminster (parish).

Westbury Hd.: Dillton.

Whorwellsdown Hd.: (Steeple) [West] Ashton and Henton, North Bradley, Edington, (Great) Hinton, Keevil, Semington and Littleton (Steeple Ashton).

Wilton Borough: South Newton [and Lowesby], *Netherhampton (in Wilton) [Prot. Ret. under Cawdon and Cadworth Hd.], Sherrington, *Wilton *See also* Branch and Dole Hd.

Taxation Records

Published: 'The Monthly Assessments for the Relief of Ireland raised in the Division of **Warminster**, 1648' [Wiltshire R.O., 413/29], *Wiltshire Archaeological Magazine*, **37** (117), 1912, pp. 353-79. Indexed.
This includes the following hundreds and places:

Damerham (South) Hd.: Damerham (tithing), Martin, (Longbridge) Deverill [Deuerell], Compton [Copton] (Chamberlayne), Monkton Deverill [Monton Dev'ell].

Dunworth Hd.: Fonthill (Gifford) (tithing), Tisbury [Tisburie], Staple, Hatch, Chisgrove, Chilmark [Chillmarke] and Ridge, Sedgehill [Sedhull], Chicklade, Teffont (Evias), Berwick (St. Leonard) [Barwicke], Swallowcliffe [Swaklie], Anstey [Anstie], Charleton, Haiston, Dognell [in Donhead], Winsford.

Mere Hd.: Mere [Meere] (tithing), Zeals, (West) Knoyle [Knoile], Charnige, Stourton [Sturton], Kingston Deverill [Deu'ell], Maiden-Bradley [Bradlie].

Wiltshire: *Taxation records* continued

Warminster Hd.: Warminster (tithing), Smallbrooke, Teffont (Magna), Boreham, Norton, Dinton, Sutton (Veny), Corsley, Upton (Scudamore), Fisherton (de la Mere) and Bapton, Bishopstrow, Norridge, (Upper) Pertwood.

Heytesbury Hd.: Codford (tithing), Chitterne, Boyton and Corton, Imber, Heytesbury [Haitsburie], Horningsham, Orcheston [Orston] (St. George), Knook(e), Brixton Deverill [Deu'rell], Hill Deverill [Hull-Deu'rell], Ashton Gifford (in Codford St. Peter), Tytherington [Tithrington], Upton Lovell, Baycliffe [Bakley] (in Horningsham), Bathampton (Battington), Whitley.

Whorwellsdown [Horrellsdowne] Hd.: Steeple Ashton (tithing), Southwick [Southweeke], Semington, Tinhead, (East) Coulston and Tilshe(a)d, (Great) Hinton, Edington, West Ashton, Keevil(l) [the roll is torn and at least one parish is missing, probably North Bradley].

Subsidy. **1641. Dunworth, Mere and South Damerham Hds.** in 'Copy of a ms. in the possession of Sir Walter Grove, bt.', to which is prefixed a copy of a lay subsidy preserved in the Public Record Office' (approx. 1,125 names) [private collection and E 179/199/407], *W.A.M.* **38**(122) (1914), pp. 589-630.
‡ = in lay subsidy only; Other places appear in both lists, except for Chadenwich.

Dunworth Hd.: Hatch, Tisbury, Staple, Chichesgrove/Chicksgrove, Anstie/Anst(e)y, ‡Chilmark [Chilmerke], Fonthill [Fountell] Gifford, Rudge, Swallowcliffe [Swallocliff], Teffont Evias, Chicklade, Sed(e)ghill, Berwick [Barwicke/Bayrwicke] St. Leonard, Winsford.

Dunworth Liberty: Dognell, Haystone, Charleton.

Me(e)re Hd.: Me(e)re towne, Me(e)re Woodlands, Sayles/Seales, St(o)urton, West Knoyle [Idire], Kingstone Deverill, Libertas Maiden Bradley, Chadenwich [in Grove list only].

Damerham South Hd.: South Damerham (tithing), ‡Martin, Compton Chamberlayne [Chamberlin], Longbridge Deverill, Monkton [Mounton] Deverill.

Downton Hd. [Knoyle Libertas]: ‡(East) Knoyle, ‡Hindon Burgus, ‡Fonthill Bishop [Fountell Episcopi].

?Assessment. **1643. Westbury Hd.** 'Return for the Hundred of Westbury, 1643', *W.A.M.* **39**(126) (1917), pp. 445-48. Tax list (62 names) [private collection]. Indexed. This includes the following places:
Penlie, Bratton, Hawridge, Leigh, Shortstreet, Dilton, Brook, Hywood, Westbury.

Public Record Office [E 179].

Subsidy, 1641:
Salisbury (350). 4 ms. [199/404].
Alderbury (120, **Amesbury** (200), **Elstub** (200) **Hds**. 5 ms. [239/207].
Alderbury (100); **Amesbury** (160); **Elstub and Everleigh** (200); **Branch and Dole** (200), some fading; **Cawden and Cadworth** (150); **Downton** (80); **Chalk** (120); **Underditch** (5); **Frustfield** (25) **Hds**. 9 ms. [259/22].
Branch and Dole (200), **Cawden** (170), **Chalk** (100), **Frustfield** (40), **Underditch** (50) **Hds**. 5 ms. [199/405].
Bradford (110), **Melksham** (130), **Westbury** (60) **Hds.**; some illegible. 2 ms. [199/415].
Chippenham (400), **Calne** (120) **Hds.**; some poor. 5 ms. [199/406].
Dunworth (175), **Mere** (99), **South Damerham** (126) **Hds**. 6 ms. [199/407]. *Published.*
Dunworth (200), **Mere** (500), **South Damerham** (200) **Hds.**, with document **1655** concerning plundering of agent. 10 ms. [259/25].
Kingsbridge (170), **Highworth** (230) **Hds**. 4 ms. [199/403].

Wiltshire: *Taxation records* continued

Assessment, 1642:
Bradford (400), **Melksham** (600), **Westbury** (400) **Hds.**; on last page, parishes of Dilton, Penleigh and Bratton, partly lost. 8 ms. [199/408].
Calne (500), **North Damerham** (250) **Hds**. 8 ms. [199/412].
Chippenham Hd. (1,000). 5 ms. [199/422].
Kinwardstone Hd. (750). 5 ms. [199/411].
Malmesbury Hd. (750), bad in parts. 8 ms. [199/409].
Swanborough Hd. (850). 5 ms. [199/410].
Swanborough Hd. (750). 6 ms. [199/414].

Wiltshire Record Office, *Trowbridge.*

Parliamentary Assessment:
1648: Warminster Division (Hds. of South Damerham, Dunworth, Heytesbury, Mere, Warminster, Whorwellsdown) [413/29]. *Published.*

See also 'Ship-money in the Hundred of **Kingsbridge**', C.W. Pugh, *W.A.M.*, **50**(178), 1943, pp. 153-69. Tax list, 1635. Not indexed. Original in library of the Wiltshire Archaeological and Natural History Society. This covers:
East Side: Wanborough, Liddington, Chiseldon, Swindon, Overtowne, Salthrop, Westlecot, Elcombe, Ufcott.
West Side: Hilmarton [Hillmerton], Tockenham Weeke, Clyffe Pypard [Cleeve Peper], Broad Town [Broadtowne], Lyneham, Preston, Tockenham, Clacke, Woodlockshaye, Lydiard [Tyddyard] Tregose and Midghall, Midghall, Wootton Bassett, Bincknoll.

Hundreds in Wiltshire are very intermingled. To keep the map simple some enclaves have been omitted.

WILTSHIRE

HIGHWORTH, CRICKLADE and STAPLE
Glos
MALMESBURY
N. DAMERHAM
KINGSBRIDGE
CHIPPENHAM
CALNE
SELKLEY
RAMSBURY
BRADFORD
MELKSHAM
POTTERNE & CANNINGS
KINWARDSTONE
WHORWELLSDOWN
SWANBOROUGH
ELSTUB & EVERLEY
WESTBURY
WARMINSTER
HEYTESBURY
AMESBURY
BRANCH & DOLE
UNDERDITCH
ALDERBURY
MERE
DUNWORTH
CAWDON and CADWORTH
W
S
DOWNTON
FRUSTFIELD
CHALKE
S. DAMERHAM

S = Salisbury
W = Wilton

WORCESTERSHIRE

Parishes: 209.

Worcestershire continued

Protestation Returns (9)

Returns are extant only for the city of Worcester. They have no signatures and marks, and women are not mentioned.

House of Lords Record Office.

Worcester (city): All Saints, St. Alban, St. Andrew, St. Clement, St. Helen, St. Martin, St. Nicholas, St. Peter, St. Swithin.

Hereford and Worcester Record Office, St. Helen's branch office, Worcester.

Stanford-on-Teme with Orleton, amongst parish records [x850 STANFORD BA 8593/1(i)].
Worcester (city). Microfilm [900.87 BA 5797] of House of Lords original; indexed transcript [899.385 BA 5219].

Collection in Aid of Protestants in Ireland (2)

Public Record Office.

Halfshire Hd.: Bromsgrove [E 179/260/2].
Oswaldslow Hd.: Hanbury [SP 28/195].

Worcestershire continued

Taxation Records

Public Record Office [E 179].

Subsidy, 1641:
Doddingtree Hd. (500). 3 ms. [201/304].
Doddingtree Hd. (400). 7 ms. [201/306].
Evesham (60) 1 m. [201/302].
"Limits of **Evesham** and **Pershore**" (500). 6 ms. [201/303].
Halfshire Hd. (600), poor in parts. 6 ms. [201/305].
Halfshire Hd. (700), poor in parts. 7 ms. [201/311].
City of **Worcester**, by wards (150), poor. 2 ms. [201/310].
City of **Worcester**, by wards (150), poor in parts. 3 ms. [201/301].
City of **Worcester**, by wards (80), some faded. 3 ms. [201/309].

Parliamentary assessment, 1647:
Doddingtree Hd. Excellent document. Contemporary but marked 'Duplicate' in preamble. Great detail. Major assessment (est. 2,000) [260/3].

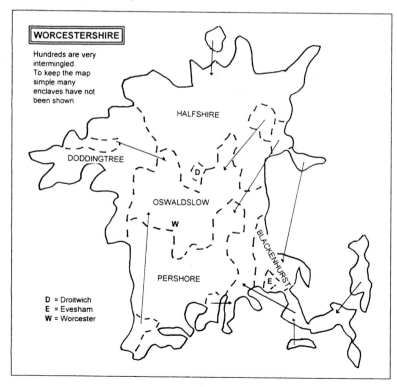

WORCESTERSHIRE

Hundreds are very intermingled.
To keep the map simple many enclaves have not been shown

HALFSHIRE

DODDINGTREE

OSWALDSLOW

PERSHORE

BLACKENHURST

D = Droitwich
E = Evesham
W = Worcester

YORKSHIRE: EAST RIDING

Taxation Records

Public Record Office [E 179].

Subsidy, 1641:
Town of **Beverley** (120). 2 ms. [205/465].
Wapentake of **Buckrose**(?), very poor. 2 ms. [205/472].
Wapentake of **Dickering** (250), fading. 5 ms. [205/478].
Wapentake of **Dickering**, mostly illegible. 3 ms. [205/483].
Wapentake of **Harthill** (200) poor. 1 m. [205/462].
Wapentake of **Harthill - Hunsley Beacon** (200). 2 ms. [205/473].
Wapentake of **Harthill - Wilton Beacon** (200), fading. 1 m. [205/474].
Wapentake of **Harthill - Wilton** (150) and **Holme** (150) **Beacons**; fading in parts. 2 ms. [205/475].
Wapentake of **Harthill - Hunsley** (200) and **Bainton** (150) **Beacons**. 3 ms. [205/479].
Wapentake of **Holderness** (550). 5 ms. [205/464].
Wapentake of **Holderness - North**; illegible. 2 ms. [205/463].

Yorkshire: East Riding: *Taxation records* contd

Wapentake of **Howdenshire** (300). 4 ms. [205/466].
Hull (60) 2 ms. [204/447].
Hull, by wards (300). 3 ms. 205/461].
Wapentake of **Ouse and Derwent** (200), fading in parts. 2 ms. [205/468].
Hull, by wards (200). 3 ms. 205/469].
Hull, by wards (180). 2 ms. [205/482].
Wapentake of **Ouse and Derwent** (150). 2 ms. [205/470].

Hull City Record Office.

Subsidy, 1641:
(Sept.). **Hull**: Whitefriar and St. Mary's Ward and Hessle [CAT 11-13].
(17 C.I): **Kingston upon Hull** (town but not county) [CAT 14].

There are no *Protestation Returns* for the East Riding of Yorkshire at the *House of Lords Record Office*; nor are there returns in the *Collection in Aid of Distressed Protestants in Ireland* at the *Public Record Office*.

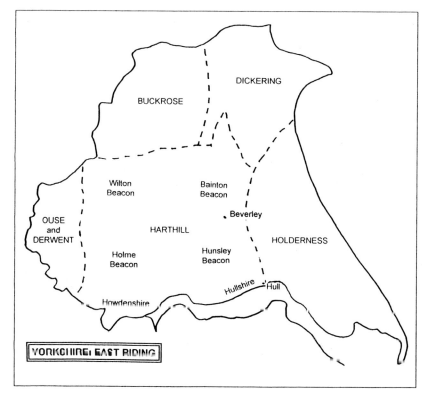

YORKSHIRE: NORTH RIDING

Returns are only extant for the Allertonshire Division, the area around Northallerton, in the middle and northern part of the North Riding. Women (§) are mentioned at Osmotherley (in family groups), some at Northallerton, and, with signatures and marks(†), at Sessy-cum-Hutton.

House of Lords Record Office.

Allertonshire Division: Birkby [Borkby]; Brompton, nigh Northallerton; Hutton Bonville, (Kirby) Sigston; Leake, Knayton, Landmoth, and Nether Silton; §**Northallerton** [North Allerton]; §Osmotherley, West Harsley, Ellerback, and Thimbleby; North Otterington; West Roun(c)ton; †§Sess(a)y-cum-Hutton [Heaton]; Thornton-le-Street; *Allertonshire Division*, clergy and officials; names of those refuse to take the protestation.

Public Record Office [E 179].

Subsidy, 1641:
Wapentake of **Allerton**, wanting. 1 m. [261/22].
Wapentake of **Birdforth** (200), parts illegible. 3 ms. [215/415].
Wapentake of **Birdforth** (170). 3 ms. [215/427].
Wapentake of **Bulmer** (300), some fading. 6 ms. [215/417].
Wapentake of **West Gilling** (120), some fading. 2 ms. [215/407].
Wapentake of **West Gilling** (120) poor. 2 ms. [215/412].

Wapentake of **West Gilling** (300), poor. 5 ms. [215/418].
Wapentake of **Hallikeld** (80), including recusants and non-communicants in parishes of Burneston and Pickhill. 2 ms. [215/413].
Wapentake of **East Hang** (100), poor. 3 ms. [215/425].
Wapentake of **East Hang** (100), only one or two per parish. 5 ms. [215/426].
Wapentake of **Langbaurgh** (est. 300), mostly illegible. 4 ms. [215/424].
Wapentake of **Langbaurgh** (certificate of defaulters) (50). No parishes. [215/428].
Wapentake of **Pickering Lythe** (160). 4 ms. [215/414].
Wapentake of **Pickering Lythe** (80), poor. 2 ms. [215/416].
Wapentake of **Ryedale** (160), some lost. 4 ms. [215/408].
Town of **Scarborough** (12). 1 m. [215/409].
Town of **Scarborough** (12). 1 m. [215/411].
Liberty of **Whitby** (150), some fading. 2 ms. [215/410].
Liberty of **Whitby** (100), fading in places. 2 ms. [215/423].

Parliamentary assessments, 1658-59:
Stokesley. Three lists (15 names each, mostly the same), dated 18 June 1658, 18 July and 16 September 1659. 3ff. [218/207].

There are no returns for the North Riding c Yorkshire in the *Collection in Aid of Distresse* *Protestants in Ireland* at the *Public Record Office.*

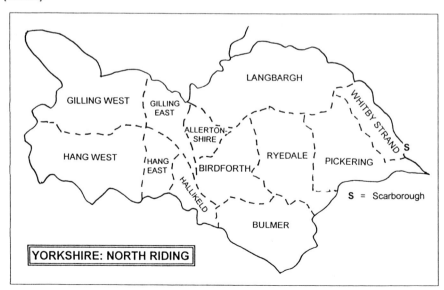

YORKSHIRE: WEST RIDING

Parishes: 261

Protestation Returns (130)

Returns are extant in quantity only for the western wapentakes of Agbrigg and Morley. These are in two sets of membranes, each in one hand throughout, thus with no signatures and marks, and women are not mentioned. The first is confined to Agbrigg, the second covers Morley and part of Agbrigg

The only other returns are for Ripon (in wards and streets) in Claro Wapentake, otherwise confined to summaries, as below; and a few places in Osgoldcross Wapentake. The main return for Pontefract has signatures and marks (†).

Published: **Morley Wapentake:** Halifax, *Halifax Antiquarian Society Transactions*, vol. **16**, edited by C.T. Clay, pp. 105-115. 1919.

House of Lords Record Office:

Agbrigg Wapentake: Ackton [Agkton], Almondbury, Al(s)tofts, Alverthorpe, East Ardsley [Ardslaw], Austonley, Batley, West Bretton, Carlton, Cartworth, Churwell, Criggleston, Crofton, Crossland-cum-Natherton and Armitage, Dewsbury, Emley, Farnley Tyas, Flockton, F(o)ulston(e), Gildsome, Golcar, Hepworth,

Agbrigg Wapentake ctd.: Holme, Honley, Horbury, Huddersfield *(typescript transcript at Local History Library, Huddersfield)*, Kirkburton, Kirkheaton, Lenthwaite, Lepton, Lindley, Lofthouse, Longwood, Marsden, Meltham-cum-Netherthong, Methley, Middleton, Mirfield, Normanton, Ossett, Oulton, Rothwell, Rothwell Haigh, Sandall, Scammonden [Skamanden], Shelley, Shepley, Shitlington, Slaithwaite, Snydall, Soothill, Stanley, Thornes, Thornhill, Thorpe, Thurstonland, Upperthong [Overthwonge], Wakefield, Walton, Warmfield, Whitley-cum-Breistwell, Whitwood, Wooldale [Woodall], Woodkirk [Woodchurch] alias West Ardsley [Westardley], Wrigglesworth; *Agbrigg Wapentake*, clergy and officials.

Morley and part of **Agbrigg Wapentake:** Adwalton, Allerton, Barkisland, Birkinshaw, Birstall, Bowling [Boulling], Bradford, Calverley, Clayton, (Cleck) Heaton, Clifton, Crosland, Cross Stone [Crostone], Drighlington, Eccleshall, Elland, Erringden, Little Gomersall, Gre(e)tland, Halifax *(published)*, Hartshead [Heartshead], Haworth, Heaton, Hec(k)mondwike, Heptonstall, Horton, Hunsworth, Illin(g)worth, Kemerseidge, Kirklees, Lightcliffe, Little Liversedge, Luddenden, Manningham, Norland, Oakenshaw, Pudsey,

Morley and Agbrigg Wapentakes continued:
Quick-cum-Saddleworth [Sudlaworth], Rastrike-cum-Fixby [Fekesby], Rishworth, Scholes, Shipley, Sowerby, Sowerby Bridge [Brigg], Soyland, Spen, Stainland, Stansfield, Taley(?), Thornton, Wadsworth, Warley, Wibsey, Wilsden, Wyke [Wike]; *Morley and part of Agbrigg Wapentake*, clergy and officials.

Claro Wapentake: Kirkby Malzeard and Middlesmoor (summary of persons taking and refusing to take the protestation), **Ripon**; *Claro Wapentake*, summary of persons who have, and also of those who refuse to take the protestation throughout the wapentake.

Osgoldcross Wapentake: East Hardwick; Ferrybridge (part); Hardwick, Tanshelf (part), Ferrybriggs (part) and Carlton; Monkhill, †Pontefract (incl. Micklegate and North Gate), Tanshelf [Tanshall] (part).

West Yorkshire Record Office, Wakefield.

Microfilm copies of West Riding returns.
Transcript of **Agbrigg Wapentake** [Z.125]. Others in progress.

Collection in Aid of Protestants in Ireland (1)

Public Record Office [SP 28/195].

Strafforth and Tickhill Wapentake: Rotherham.

Taxation Records

Public Record Office [E 179].

Subsidy, 1641:
Wapentakes of **Agbrigg** (400), **Morley** (400). 5 ms. [209/363].
Wapentakes of **Agbrigg** (400), **Morley** (400); poor in places. 6 ms. [209/367].
Wapentake of **Claro** (1,100), some fading. 8 ms. [209/364].
Wapentake of **Claro** (1,200), some fading. 8 ms. [262/8].
Wapentake of **Claro** (600). 12 ms. [209/379].
Wapentake of **Osgoldcross** (800), poor in places. 4 ms. [209/366].
Wapentake of **Osgoldcross** (600), some fading. 4 ms. [209/370].
Wapentake of **Staincross** (300). 2 ms. Same date as next [209/368].
Wapentake of **Staincross** (230). 2 ms. [209/369].
Wapentake of **Strafforth and Tickhill** (850), some fading. 5 ms. [209/365].

Also others, Charles I, not examined; mostly imperfect [209/375-384 (excl.379)].

YORK CITY and the AINSTY

Parishes: 30.

Protestation Returns (3)

Borthwick Institute of Historical Research, York (see *A Guide to Parish Records in the Borthwick Institute of Historical Research*, C.C. Webb, 1988).

York: St. Denys with St. George [PR Y/DEN. 1], St. Margaret Walmage [PR Y/MARG. 2], St. Saviour [PR Y/SAV. 1A] [in parish registers].

There are no *Protestation Returns* for the City of York and the Ainsty at the *House of Lords Record Office*.

Collection in Aid of Protestants in Ireland (17)

Public Record Office [SP 28/195].

Ainsty: Acomb [originally filed under Bucks., SP 28/191], Askham Richard, Bolton Percy.
York (city): All Saints in North Street, All Saints of the Pavement, Holy Trinity Goodramgate, St. Helen Stonegate, St. John Delpike, St. John at Ousebridge, St. Martin in Coney Street, St. Mary Bishopshill the Younger, St. Maurice in Monkgate, St. Michael at Ousebridge, St. Olive's near the Wall, St. Peter the Little, St. Saviour, St. Wilfrid.

Taxation Returns

Public Record Office [E 179].

Subsidy, 1641:
City, by wards (250), bad in places. 2 ms. [218/205].
City, by wards (250), fading, bad in places. 2 ms. [218/209].
Ainsty (130), poor in places. 1m. [218/206].
Ainsty (100), fading. 1 m. [218/210].

Assessment, 1642:
City - Bootham ward (350), fading. 3 ms. [218/208].
City - Monk ward (60), poor. 2 ms. [218/204].

Certificates of deaths and removals:
1649. City - Monk ward. By parish within ward (250+), listed 'these are poor and have no goods', 'these are dead', 'these are absent or removed from said parish'. 4 ms. [218/212].
1650. City - Walmgate ward. By parish within ward (350+), listed as 'these are dead', 'these are gone away', 'these are poore', these are moved out of the said ward'. 4 ms. [218/207].

WALES

The only extant returns for Wales are those for the three Denbighshire boroughs.

Published: **Denbighshire:** in *Hel Achau* (Clwyd FHS Journal), introduction, **2** (1980), p. 27; Denbigh (borough), **4** (1981), pp. 7-9; Holt (borough), **6** (1982), pp. 11-14; Ruthin (borough), **12** (1984), pp. 18-21.

House of Lords Record Office.

Holdings as published, above.

No other returns for Wales (or Monmouthshire) are held by the *House of Lords Record Office.*

Collection in Aid of Protestants in Ireland

Public Record Office [E 179/265/11].

Pembrokeshire: Haverfordwest: St. Martin, St. Mary, St. Thomas.

No other returns for Wales are in the *Collection in Aid of Distressed Protestants in Ireland.*

Taxation Records

Public Record Office [E 179].

Subsidy, 1641:

Anglesey
By Hd. only (150). 2 ms. [219/23].

Breconshire
Too fragile to examine. 5 ms. [263/25].

Wales: *Subsidy, 1641* continued

Caernarvonshire
By Hd. only (200). 2 ms. [220/158].
By Hd. only (270), fading. 2 ms. [220/159].

Cardiganshire
Hds. of **Ilar** (150), **Llanbadarn-Fawr** (60), **Moyddyn** (80), **Penarth** (50), **Troedyraur** (90). 4 ms. [219/89].
Hd. of **Ilar** (120), very poor. 4 ms. [263/42].
Hds. of **Troedyraur** (50), **Moyddynn** and **Cardigan** (100). 3 ms. [219/89a].

Carmarthenshire
County? (500), very faded. 4 ms. [264/14].

Denbighshire
By Hd. only. Hds. of **Bromfield** (150), **Chirk** (80, **Isaled** (80), **Isdulas** (60), **Ruthin** (80), **Yale** (20), Borough. of **Denbigh** (50). 4 ms. [221/204].

Montgomeryshire
Hds. of **Llanidloes, Newtown, Montgomery** and **Machynlleth** (250). 5 ms. [223/402].

Pembrokeshire
Haverfordwest (40). 1 m. [224/523].
Haverfordwest (40), very poor. 1 m. [224/523a]

Radnorshire
County (fragmented), not counted. 4 ms. [224/589].
Hd. of **Rhaiader** (40), fragment. 2 ms. [239/239].

Assessment, 1642(?):

Breconshire
County. By hundred and parish (1,200). A major listing. 10 ms. [263/26].